AF575833

TO

FROM

FAITH *of* AMERICA

250

PRAYERS FOR OUR NATION

An Imprint of Thomas Nelson

INTRODUCTION

From its very beginning, America has been a nation shaped by prayer, guiding its leaders and citizens through times of triumph and challenge.

George Washington bowed a knee in *The Prayer at Valley Forge.* This famous painting depicts the father of our country going to God in prayer when he, his troops, and our nation faced a crisis during the Revolutionary War.

During the Civil War, President Lincoln declared March 30, 1863, a National Day of Prayer. "We have become . . . too proud to pray to the God that made us," Lincoln said at the time. "It behooves us, then, to humble ourselves before the offended Power, to confess our national sins, and to pray for clemency and forgiveness." Lincoln delivered his Second Inaugural Address on April 10, 1865, to a broken nation: "Fondly do we hope—fervently do we pray—that this mighty scourge of war may speedily pass away. Yet, if God wills that it continue . . . so still it must be said 'the judgments of the Lord, are true and righteous altogether.'"

Recognizing the enduring power of prayer, in 1952, President Truman established the annual National Day of Prayer—a tradition that continues to bring hope and unity to our nation.

Throughout America's history, men and women have turned to God's Word for wisdom, strength, and encouragement, building their lives on God's promises. Our early leaders' faith and dependence on God laid the moral and spiritual foundation that still holds our nation together.

A PRAYER FOR OUR LEADERS

To the distinguished Character of Patriot, it should be our highest Glory to add the more distinguished Character of Christian.

—George Washington

O Lord our Governor, whose glory is in all the world: We commend this nation to thy merciful care, that, being guided by thy Providence, we may dwell secure in thy peace. Grant to the President of the United States, the Governor of this State (or Commonwealth), and to all in authority, wisdom and strength to know and to do thy will. Fill them with the love of truth and righteousness, and make them ever mindful of their calling to serve this people in thy fear; through Jesus Christ our Lord, who liveth and reigneth with thee and the Holy Spirit, one God, world without end. Amen.

—THE BOOK OF COMMON PRAYER

PRAYER

Father God, I lift our nation's leaders to You today. I ask You to guide and direct them. Amen.

A BRAVE RESISTANCE

I learned that courage was not the absence of fear, but the triumph over it. The brave man is not he who does not feel afraid, but he who conquers that fear.

—Nelson Mandela

On July 2, 1776, the Continental Congress in Philadelphia declared independence from Great Britain. Meanwhile, on Long Island, George Washington, commander in chief of the Continental Army, gathered his troops and wrote in the General Orders that we, as a nation, serve under God.

The time is now near at hand which must probably determine, whether Americans are to be, Freemen, or Slaves. . . . The fate of unborn Millions will now depend, under God, on the Courage and Conduct of this army—Our cruel and unrelenting Enemy leaves us no choice but a brave resistance, or the most abject submission; this is all we can expect. . . . The Eyes of all our Countrymen are now upon us, and we shall have their blessings, and praises, if happily we are the instruments of saving them from the Tyranny meditated against them. . . . Let us therefore . . . shew the whole world, that a Freeman contending for Liberty on his own ground is superior to any slavish mercenary on earth.

PRAYER

Lord, thank You for giving us leaders who gave our great nation the strength to endure. Amen.

GLORIFYING THE FATHER

Within the covers of that single Book [the Bible] are all the answers to all the problems that face us today. . . . The Bible can touch our hearts, order our minds, refresh our souls.

—Ronald Reagan

That the Father may be glorified in the Son [John 14:13]. It is to this end that Jesus on His throne in glory will do everything we ask in His Name. Every answer to prayer He gives will have this as its object. When there is no prospect of this object being obtained, He will not answer. It follows as a matter of course that with us, as with Jesus, this must be the essential element in our petitions. The glory of the Father must be the aim—the very soul and life—of our prayer.

—ANDREW MURRAY

PRAYER

Lord, help us as a nation to discern right from wrong, so our moral voices may bring honor and glory to You. Amen.

THE SPIRIT'S HELP

Wish not so much to live long as to live well.

—Benjamin Franklin

We do not know how to pray as we ought" for two reasons. First, it is not yet clear what future we are hoping for or where we are heading, and second, many things in this life may seem positive but are in fact negative, and vice versa. Tribulation, for example, when it comes to a servant of God in order to test or correct him may seem futile to those who have less understanding. . . . But God often helps us through tribulation, and prosperity, which may be negative if it traps the soul with delight and the love of this life, is sought after in vain. The Spirit sighs by making us sigh, arousing in us by his love a desire for the future life. "The Lord your God tempts you so that he might know whether you love him," that is, to make you know, for nothing escapes God's notice.

—SAINT AUGUSTINE

PRAYER

Lord, I don't always know how to pray. Thank You for Your Spirit, who prays through me. Amen.

PRAYING TO A GOD WHO ACTS

Why is it that next to the birthday of the Savior of the World, your most joyous and most venerated festival returns on this day [July 4th]?

—John Adams

To say, "Father, I should like this or that," would be enough at once, if the wish were bad, to make us know it and turn from it. Such prayer about things must of necessity help to bring the mind into true and simple relation with him; to make us remember his will even when we do not see what that will is. Surely it is better and more trusting to tell him all without fear or anxiety. Was it not thus the Lord carried himself towards his Father when he said, "If it be possible, let this cup pass from me"? . . . There is no apprehension that God might be displeased with him for saying what he would like, and not leaving it all to his Father. Neither did he regard his Father's plans as necessarily so fixed that they could not be altered to his prayer.

—GEORGE MACDONALD

PRAYER

God, please help me see Your will in my situation today. Amen.

THE BIRTH OF A NATION

We hold these truths to be self-evident, that all men are created equal, that they are endowed by their Creator with certain unalienable Rights, that among these are Life, Liberty and the pursuit of Happiness.

—Declaration of Independence

In May 1775, tension crackled in Philadelphia. The thirteen colonies, weary of British rule—unjust taxes, trade limits, voiceless laws—sent representatives to the Second Continental Congress. After several attempts to seek a peaceful resolution with Great Britain, the Congress decided to formally declare the colonies' independence from the world's most powerful empire.

Thomas Jefferson, John Adams, and Benjamin Franklin struggled to find language that could spark a revolution. Jefferson declared that all are created equal, with unalienable rights—life, liberty, and the pursuit of happiness. From this principle, they insisted governments must defend these rights; if violated, people must overthrow tyrants.

The document listed grievances against King George III: taxes without consent, dissolved legislatures, unjust trials, and armies on their soil. Each complaint told a story of oppression. As resentment grew, the colonists' resolve was fueled.

On July 4, 1776, the Continental Congress adopted the Declaration of Independence. The United States of America emerged on the world stage, advancing a message of liberty that would inspire generations.

PRAYER

Lord, give me the courage to stand with my fellow Americans when faced with evil that goes against Your Word. Amen.

IN CONGRESS, JULY 4, 1776

The unanimous Declaration of the thirteen united States of America, When in the Course of human events, it becomes necessary for one people to dissolve the political bands which have connected them with another, and to assume among the powers of the earth, the separate and equal station to which the Laws of Nature and of Nature's God entitle them, a decent respect to the opinions of mankind requires that they should declare the causes which impel them to the separation.

We hold these truths to be self-evident, that all men are created equal, that they are endowed by their Creator with certain unalienable Rights, that among these are Life, Liberty and the pursuit of Happiness.—That to secure these rights, Governments are instituted among Men, deriving their just powers from the consent of the governed, —That whenever any Form of Government becomes destructive of these ends, it is the Right of the People to alter or to abolish it, and to institute new Government, laying its foundation on such principles and organizing its powers in such form, as to them shall seem most likely to effect their Safety and Happiness. Prudence, indeed, will dictate that Governments long established should not be changed for light and transient causes; and accordingly all experience hath shewn, that mankind are more disposed to suffer, while evils are sufferable, than to right themselves by abolishing the forms to which they are accustomed. But when a long train of abuses and usurpations, pursuing invariably the same Object evinces a design to reduce them under absolute Despotism, it is their right, it is their duty, to throw off such Government, and to provide new Guards for their future security.—Such has been the patient sufferance of these Colonies; and such is now the necessity which constrains them to alter their former Systems of Government. The history of the present King of Great Britain is a history of repeated injuries and usurpations, all having in direct object the establishment of an absolute Tyranny over these States. To prove this, let Facts be submitted to a candid world.

He has refused his Assent to Laws, the most wholesome and necessary for the public good.

He has forbidden his Governors to pass Laws of immediate and pressing importance, unless suspended in their operation till his Assent should be obtained; and when so suspended, he has utterly neglected to attend to them.

He has refused to pass other Laws for the accommodation of large districts of people, unless those people would relinquish the right of Representation in the Legislature, a right inestimable to them and formidable to tyrants only.

He has called together legislative bodies at places unusual, uncomfortable, and distant from the depository of their public Records, for the sole purpose of fatiguing them into compliance with his measures.

He has dissolved Representative Houses repeatedly, for opposing with manly firmness his invasions on the rights of the people.

He has refused for a long time, after such dissolutions, to cause others to be elected; whereby the Legislative powers, incapable of Annihilation, have returned to the People at large for their exercise; the State remaining in the mean time exposed to all the dangers of invasion from without, and convulsions within.

He has endeavoured to prevent the population of these States; for that purpose obstructing the Laws for Naturalization of Foreigners; refusing to pass others to encourage their migrations hither, and raising the conditions of new Appropriations of Lands.

He has obstructed the Administration of Justice, by refusing his Assent to Laws for establishing Judiciary powers.

He has made Judges dependent on his Will alone, for the tenure of their offices, and the amount and payment of their salaries.

He has erected a multitude of New Offices, and sent hither swarms of Officers to harrass our people, and eat out their substance.

He has kept among us, in times of peace, Standing Armies without the Consent of our legislatures.

He has affected to render the Military independent of and superior to the Civil power.

He has combined with others to subject us to a jurisdiction foreign to our constitution, and unacknowledged by our laws; giving his Assent to their Acts of pretended Legislation:

For Quartering large bodies of armed troops among us:

For protecting them, by a mock Trial, from punishment for any Murders which they should commit on the Inhabitants of these States:

For cutting off our Trade with all parts of the world:

For imposing Taxes on us without our Consent:

For depriving us in many cases, of the benefits of Trial by Jury:

For transporting us beyond Seas to be tried for pretended offences:

For abolishing the free System of English Laws in a neighbouring Province, establishing therein an Arbitrary government, and enlarging its Boundaries so as to render it at once an example and fit instrument for introducing the same absolute rule into these Colonies:

For taking away our Charters, abolishing our most valuable Laws, and altering fundamentally the Forms of our Governments:

For suspending our own Legislatures, and declaring themselves invested with power to legislate for us in all cases whatsoever.

He has abdicated Government here, by declaring us out of his Protection and waging War against us.

He has plundered our seas, ravaged our Coasts, burnt our towns, and destroyed the lives of our people.

He is at this time transporting large Armies of foreign Mercenaries to compleat the works of death, desolation and tyranny, already begun with circumstances of Cruelty & perfidy scarcely paralleled in the most barbarous ages, and totally unworthy the Head of a civilized nation.

He has constrained our fellow Citizens taken Captive on the high Seas to bear Arms against their Country, to become the executioners of their friends and Brethren, or to fall themselves by their Hands.

He has excited domestic insurrections amongst us, and has endeavoured to bring on the inhabitants of our frontiers, the merciless Indian Savages, whose known rule of warfare, is an undistinguished destruction of all ages, sexes and conditions.

In every stage of these Oppressions We have Petitioned for Redress in the most humble terms: Our repeated Petitions have been answered only by repeated injury. A Prince, whose character is thus marked by every act which may define a Tyrant, is unfit to be the ruler of a free people.

Nor have We been wanting in attentions to our Brittish brethren. We have warned them from time to time of attempts by their legislature to extend an unwarrantable jurisdiction over us. We have reminded them of the circumstances of our emigration and settlement here. We have appealed to their native justice and magnanimity, and we have conjured them by the ties of our common kindred to disavow these usurpations, which, would inevitably interrupt our connections and correspondence. They too have been deaf to the voice of justice and of consanguinity. We must, therefore, acquiesce in the necessity, which denounces our Separation, and hold them, as we hold the rest of mankind, Enemies in War, in Peace Friends.

We, therefore, the Representatives of the united States of America, in General Congress, Assembled, appealing to the Supreme Judge of the world for the rectitude of our intentions, do, in the Name, and by Authority of the good People of these Colonies, solemnly publish and declare, That these United Colonies are, and of Right ought to be Free and Independent States; that they are Absolved from all Allegiance to the British Crown, and that all political connection between them and the State of Great Britain, is and ought to be totally dissolved; and that as Free and Independent States, they have full Power to levy War, conclude Peace, contract Alliances, establish Commerce, and to do all other

Acts and Things which Independent States may of right do. And for the support of this Declaration, with a firm reliance on the protection of divine Providence, we mutually pledge to each other our Lives, our Fortunes and our sacred Honor.

Georgia
Button Gwinnett
Lyman Hall
George Walton
North Carolina
William Hooper
Joseph Hewes
John Penn
South Carolina
Edward Rutledge
Thomas Heyward, Jr.
Thomas Lynch, Jr.
Arthur Middleton
Massachusetts
John Hancock
Maryland
Samuel Chase
William Paca
Thomas Stone
Charles Carroll of Carrollton
Virginia
George Wythe
Richard Henry Lee
Thomas Jefferson
Benjamin Harrison
Thomas Nelson, Jr.
Francis Lightfoot Lee
Carter Braxton
Pennsylvania
Robert Morris
Benjamin Rush
Benjamin Franklin
John Morton
George Clymer
James Smith
George Taylor
James Wilson
George Ross
Delaware
Caesar Rodney
George Read
Thomas McKean
New York
William Floyd
Philip Livingston
Francis Lewis
Lewis Morris
New Jersey
Richard Stockton
John Witherspoon
Francis Hopkinson
John Hart
Abraham Clark
New Hampshire
Josiah Bartlett
William Whipple
Massachusetts
Samuel Adams
John Adams
Robert Treat Paine
Elbridge Gerry
Rhode Island
Stephen Hopkins
William Ellery
Connecticut
Roger Sherman
Samuel Huntington
William Williams
Oliver Wolcott
New Hampshire
Matthew Thornton

GOD ALONE

Prayer will make a man cease from sin, or sin will entice a man to cease from prayer. . . . Pray often, for prayer is a shield to the soul, a sacrifice to God and a scourge for Satan.

—John Bunyan

Devotion is neither private nor public prayer; but prayers, whether private or public, are particular parts or instances of devotion. Devotion signifies a life given, or devoted, to God.

He, therefore, is the devout man, who lives no longer to his own will, or the way and spirit of the world, but to the sole will of God, who considers God in everything, who serves God in everything, who makes all the parts of his common life parts of piety, by doing everything in the Name of God, and under such rules as are conformable to His glory.

We readily acknowledge, that God alone is to be the rule and measure of our prayers, that in them we are to look wholly unto Him, and act wholly for Him; that we are only to pray in such a manner, for such things, and such ends, as are suitable to His glory.

—ADAPTED FROM WILLIAM LAW

PRAYER

Lord, I pray for myself and for our country that we humbly come to You with full devotion. Amen.

TRUE ASSURANCE

Prayer is not monologue, but dialogue. Its most essential part is God's voice in response to mine.

—Andrew Murray

I think the first essential mark of the difference between true and false assurance is to be found in the fact that the true works humility. There is nothing in the world that works such satanic, profound, God-defiant pride as false assurance; nothing works such utter humility, or brings to such utter self-emptiness, as the child-like spirit of true assurance. Surely this can be known. If a person is self-confident, there is self-assurance; if there is any evidence of pride in connection with his claim, it is a most deadly mark—it is the plague-spot which marks death and corruption. But if there is utter humility, you have the sign of the true spirit.

—A. A. HODGE

PRAYER

Father, I am so grateful of the assurance You have given to me of my salvation! Amen.

HOLD ON

Having thus chosen our course, without guile, and with pure purpose, let us renew our trust in God, and go forward without fear, and with manly hearts.

—Abraham Lincoln

An answer to prayer is conditional upon the amount of faith that goes to the petition. To test this, He delays the answer. The superficial pray-er subsides into silence, when the answer is delayed. But the man of prayer hangs on, and on. The Lord recognizes and honors his faith, and gives him a rich and abundant answer to his faith-evidencing, importunate prayer.

—E. M. BOUNDS

PRAYER

Lord, when I can't hold on any longer, give me the strength to reach out to You and You only. Amen.

THE TEMPLE OF THE LORD

Your prayers at the best are nothing but a beggar's cry. You still stand as beggars at the gate of mercy, asking for the dole of God's charity, for the love of Jesus. And he gives freely.

—Charles Spurgeon

Secure your interest in Christ; make it your great business, your work, your heaven, to secure your interest in Christ. This is not an age, an hour, for a man to be between fears and hopes, between doubting and believing.

Take not up in a name to live, when you are dead God-ward and Christ-ward; take not up in an outward form, and outward privilege. They cried out, "The temple of the Lord, the temple of the Lord," that had no interest in, or love to, the Lord of the temple. Follow God, leave no means unattempted whereby your blessed interest may be cleared up.

—THOMAS BROOKS

PRAYER

Lord, I call out to You for my loved ones and for our nation! Hear my prayers that they might know You more. Amen.

A PURE HEART

The welfare of America, the cause of civilization will forever require the contribution of some part of the life of all our citizens to the natural, the necessary, and the inevitable demand for the defense of the right and the truth.

— **Calvin Coolidge**

If your desire and aim is to reach the destination of the path and home of true happiness, of grace and glory, by a straight and safe way then earnestly apply your mind to seek constant purity of heart, clarity of mind, and calm of the senses. Gather up your heart's desire and fix it continually on the Lord God above. To do so you must withdraw yourself so far as you can from friends and from everyone else, and from the activities that hinder you from such a purpose. . . .

Simplify your heart with all care, diligence and effort so that still and at peace from the products of the imagination you can turn round and remain always in the Lord within yourself, as if your mind were already in the now of eternity, that is of the godhead. In this way you will be able to . . . commit yourself completely and fully to God in all difficulties and eventualities, and be willing to submit yourself patiently to his will and good pleasure at all times.

—SAINT ALBERT THE GREAT

PRAYER

Lord, I pray that You would make my heart pure before You. Amen.

SACRED IMPORTANCE

The Scriptures alone are the foundation of our beliefs as Christians. I stand on the Word of God as recorded in the Bible.

—Adapted from Martin Luther

It is interesting to remark how large a portion of Sacred Writ is occupied with the subject of prayer, either in furnishing examples, enforcing precepts, or pronouncing promises.

We scarcely open the Bible before we read, "Then began men to call upon the name of the Lord;" and just as we are about to close the volume, the "Amen" of an earnest supplication meets our ear. Instances are plentiful.

Here we find a wrestling Jacob—there a Daniel who prayed three times a day—and a David who with all his heart called upon his God. On the mountain we see Elias; in the dungeon Paul and Silas. We have multitudes of commands, and myriads of promises.

What does this teach us, but the sacred importance and necessity of prayer? We may be certain that whatever God has made prominent in his Word, he intended to be conspicuous in our lives. If he has said much about prayer, it is because he knows we have much need of it.

So deep are our necessities, that until we are in heaven we must not cease to pray.

—CHARLES SPURGEON

PRAYER

Lord, may I never cease to pray! Amen.

THE NECESSITY OF PRAYER

A prosperous state makes a secure Christian, but adversity makes him Consider.

—Anne Bradstreet

Words fail to explain how necessary prayer is. . . . Surely, with good reason the Heavenly Father affirms that the only stronghold of safety is in calling upon his name [cf. Joel 2:32]. By so doing we invoke the presence both of his providence, through which he watches over and guards our affairs, and of his power, through which he sustains us, weak as we are and well-nigh overcome, and of his goodness, through which he receives us, miserably burdened with sins, unto grace; and, in short, it is by prayer that we call him to reveal himself as wholly present to us. Hence comes an extraordinary peace and repose to our consciences. For having disclosed to the Lord the necessity that was pressing upon us, we even rest fully in the thought that none of our ills is hid from him who, we are convinced, has both the will and the power to take the best care of us.

—JOHN CALVIN

PRAYER

Lord, I turn over all my needs to You. I trust in You to care for me. Amen.

FROM THE HEART

He who permits himself to tell a lie once, finds it much easier to do it a second and third time, till at length it becomes habitual, he tells lies without attending to it, and truths without the world's believing him. This falsehood of the tongue leads to that of the heart, and in time depraves all its good dispositions.

—Thomas Jefferson

True prayer is only another name for the love of God. Its excellence does not consist in the multitude of our words; for our Father knoweth what things we have need of before we ask Him. The true prayer is that of the heart, and the heart prays only for what it desires. *To pray*, then is *to desire*—but to desire what God would have us desire. He who asks what he does not from the bottom of his heart desire, is mistaken in thinking that he prays. Let him spend days in reciting prayers, in meditation or in inciting himself to pious exercises, he prays not once truly, if he really desire not the things he pretends to ask.

—FRANÇOIS FÉNELON

PRAYER

Lord, I want Your will to become my own. Help me always to pray truly, from my heart. Amen.

SIMPLICITY IN PRAYER

The people are responsible for the character of their Congress. If that body be ignorant, reckless, and corrupt, it is because the people tolerate ignorance, recklessness, and corruption.

—James A. Garfield

Every teacher knows the power of example. He not only tells the child what to do and how to do it, but *shows* him how it really can be done. Realizing our weakness, our heavenly Teacher has given us the very words we are to take with us as we draw near to our Father. We have in them a form of prayer which contains the freshness and fullness of the Eternal Life. It is so simple that a child can say it, and so divinely rich that it encompasses all that God can give. A model and inspiration for all other prayer, it draws us at the same time back to itself as the deepest utterance of our souls before God.

—ANDREW MURRAY

PRAYER

Our Father in heaven, hallowed be Your name. May Your kingdom come and Your will be done in our nation as it is in heaven. Amen.

RESTING IN PRAYER

In times of public calamity, . . . it is especially becoming, that the hearts of all should be touched with [prayer], and the eyes of all be turned to that Almighty Power, in whose hand are the welfare and the destiny of nations.

—James Madison

I cannot help the thought which grows steadily upon me . . . that the better part of prayer is not the asking, but the kneeling where we can ask, the resting there, the staying there, drawing out the willing moments in heavenly communion with God, within the closet, with the night changed into the brightness of the day by the light of Him who all the night was in prayer to God. Just to be there, at leisure from ourselves, at leisure from the world, with our souls at liberty, with our spirit feeling its kinship to the Divine Spirit, with our life finding itself in the life of God—this is prayer. Would it be possible that one could be thus with God, listening to Him, speaking to Him, reposing upon His love, and not come out with a shining face, a gladdened heart, an intent more constant and more strong to give to the waiting world which so sadly needs what has been taken from the heart of God?

—ALEXANDER MCKENZIE

PRAYER

Lord, encourage me and strengthen me to share Your love with lost people in our nation and world. Amen.

RED, WHITE, AND BLUE

When we honor our flag we honor what we stand for as a Nation—freedom, equality, justice, and hope.

—Ronald Reagan

In the bustling streets of Philadelphia during the Revolutionary War, a skilled upholsterer named Betsy Ross worked quietly in her small shop. Known for her fine needlework and strong patriotism, Betsy's life changed when, according to popular legend, she received a visit in 1776 from George Washington, Robert Morris, and George Ross—members of a secret committee from the Continental Congress.

They brought a sketch of a new flag for the emerging nation. The colonies were on the brink of declaring independence, and they needed a symbol to unite their cause. Betsy examined the design and suggested a practical change: replacing the proposed six-pointed stars with five-pointed ones, which were easier to cut and sew. Her suggestion was accepted, and she carefully stitched the first American flag—thirteen red and white stripes for the colonies and thirteen white stars in a circle on a blue field, representing unity and equality among the states.

While historians debate the exact details of the story, Betsy Ross's role as a talented seamstress and devoted patriot became a cherished American legend.

PRAYER

Lord, I pray that each person in this country will use their God-given gifts to further Your kingdom. Amen.

DEVOTIONAL DIVERSITY

The principles of the revolution ought never to be forgotten by those who wish to preserve the blessings of freedom.

—Adapted from Mercy Otis Warren

There are some people who think that devotion will slip away from them if they relax a little. . . . Yet there are many circumstances in which as I have said, it is permissible for us to take some recreation, in order that we may be the stronger when we return to prayer.

Do not spend all of your time in one method of prayer. You may have found an excellent method of prayer that you really enjoy. Maybe you need a kind of Sunday. I mean a time of rest from your spiritual labor.

You think you would lose something if you stop working at prayer. My view is that your loss would be gain. Try to imagine yourself in the presence of Christ. Talk with him. Delight in him. There is no need to weary yourself by composing speeches to him.

There is a time for one thing and a time for another. The soul can become weary of eating the same food over and over again. There is a great variety of food that is wholesome and nutritious. If your spiritual palate becomes familiar with their various tastes, they will sustain the life of your soul, bringing many benefits.

—ADAPTED FROM SAINT TERESA OF AVILA

PRAYER

Dear God, make my prayer as natural as breathing. Amen.

MORNING PRAYER

By joint resolution of the Congress approved April 17, 1952, the recognition of . . . a National Day of Prayer has become a beloved national tradition. Now, Therefore, I . . . do hereby proclaim May 5, 1988, as a National Day of Prayer. I call upon the citizens of our great Nation to gather together on that day in homes and places of worship to pray, each after his or her own manner, for unity in the hearts of all mankind.

—**Ronald Reagan**

There are some useful short kinds of prayer. One of them is morning prayer. It is a way to prepare for the day's activities. Here is how it is done.

1. Begin by really adoring God. Thank him for preserving you through the night.
2. Acknowledge that this day is given to you as another opportunity to prepare for eternity.
3. Look for chances to serve God today. . . . Resolve to make the best of every opportunity to serve God and increase devotion that comes your way. Prepare carefully to avoid, resist, and overcome harmful things.
4. Then be humble before God. Admit that you can't do any of this on your own. Offer all of your good intentions to God, as though you were holding out your heart in your hands. Ask him to be involved in your plans for the day.

—ADAPTED FROM SAINT FRANCIS DE SALES

PRAYER

Lord, I pray that our country will renew itself to daily prayer. Amen.

PRAYER IN A TIME OF NEED

God never did anything to me that wasn't for me.

—Elisabeth Elliot

It is a great matter when, in extreme need, one can lay hold on Prayer. I know that so often as I have earnestly prayed, I have been richly heard, and have obtained more than I have prayed for. Indeed, God sometimes deferred the matter, nevertheless He came.

Oh! How great an upright and godly Christian's Prayer is! how powerful with God!

That a poor human creature should speak with God's high majesty in heaven, and not be affrighted, but know, on the contrary, that God smileth friendly upon him for Christ's sake, His dearly beloved Son!—What a wonder is this!

—MARTIN LUTHER

PRAYER

Lord, when I am in difficulty, hear my prayers. Amen.

THE GREATEST OF THESE

Oh! It is a glorious fact, that prayers are noticed in heaven.

—Charles Spurgeon

Love is the everlasting grace that will continue in use and increase, even when other graces will have ceased. Some graces are particularly suited to our present state of imperfection in this world. At the present time, we live by faith, repent and mourn for sin, live in hope of the glory which will be revealed, and wait until we possess the mansions above. We patiently wait for all the good that is promised to us but not yet conferred upon us.

However, in the future, faith will be turned into sight, hope into enjoyment, desires into gratification, and waiting into possession. When this happens, we will believe no more, nope no more, desire no more, and wait no more.

But even then we will continue in love. Indeed, we will love more than ever, more abundantly, perfectly, and continually, without pause or alternation. We will love eternally.

One reason why love is considered the greatest of the three Christian virtues, is that it will last the longest.

—ADAPTED FROM THOMAS DOOLITTLE

PRAYER

Lord, give me a servant's heart so that I desire nothing more than You! Amen.

FREEDOM AND OPPORTUNITY

Those who expect to reap the blessing of Freedom, must, like men, undergo the fatigue of supporting it.

—Thomas Paine

Booker T. Washington (1856–1915) was an educator and leader whose Christian faith and love of America shaped his ideas about progress. Born into slavery, he endured oppression, yet his faith in God gave him purpose. He often spoke about prayer, hard work, and moral character, believing spiritual strength fueled personal and community growth. Washington stressed humility, forgiveness, and service, all rooted in his Christian beliefs.

Washington cared about America. He saw its flaws but also its promise of freedom and opportunity. Instead of harboring resentment, he worked to unite Black and White Americans. At Tuskegee Institute, he promoted practical education, moral growth, and economic independence so African Americans could contribute to society. In his "Atlanta Compromise" speech in 1895, he said, "In all things that are purely social we can be as separate as the fingers, yet one as the hand in all things essential to mutual progress." This reflected his belief that unity could bring lasting change. His faith and patriotism fueled his lifelong effort to help his people and strengthen the nation.

PRAYER

Lord, may our nation be united for the good of humanity. Amen.

STAND OR FALL

Relying on God has to begin all over again every day as if nothing had yet been done.

—C. S. Lewis

The following statement by American statesman Daniel Webster was made in the nineteenth century, a time of great debate about faith versus reason and the historical reliability of religious texts:

The Gospel is either true history, or it is a consummate fraud; it is either a reality or an imposition. Christ was what he professed to be, or he was an imposter. There is no other alternative. His spotless life in his earnest enforcement of the truth, his suffering in its defense, forbids us to suppose that he was suffering an illusion of the heated brain.

Every act of his pure and holy life shows that he was the author of truth, the advocate of truth, the earnest defender of truth, and the uncomplaining sufferer for truth. Now, considering the purity of his doctrines, the simplicity of his life, and the sublimity of his death, is it possible that he would have died for an illusion? In all his preaching the Saviour made no popular appeals. His discourses were all directed to the individual. Christ and his Apostles sought to impress upon every man the conviction that he must stand or fall alone—he must live for himself and die for himself, and give up his account to the omniscient God, as though he were the only dependent creature in the Universe. The Gospel leaves the individual sinner alone with himself and his God. To his own master he stands or falls.

PRAYER

Lord, give me strength to stand on Your Word and Your Word alone. Amen.

A PRAYER FOR A DEEPER WALK

During the Great Depression, on March 4, 1933, President Franklin D. Roosevelt delivered his First Inaugural Address, famously stating, "Let me assert my firm belief that the only thing we have to fear is fear itself. . . . We face the arduous days that lie before us in the warm courage of national unity; with the clear consciousness of seeking old and precious moral values." Seeking God's blessing, the president added, "May He protect each and every one of us. May He guide me in the days to come."

Lord Jesus, take from us now everything that would hinder the closest communion with God. Any wish or desire that might hamper us in prayer remove, we pray Thee. Any memory of either sorrow or care that might hinder the fixing of our affection wholly on our God, take it away now. What have we to do with idols any more? Thou hast seen and observed us. Thou knowest where the difficulty lies. Help us against it, and may we now come boldly, not into the Holy place alone, but into the Holiest of all, where we should not dare to come if our great Lord had not rent the veil, sprinkled the mercy seat with His own blood, and bidden us enter.

—CHARLES SPURGEON

PRAYER

Father, I pray that our nation stays strong in understanding Your truth. Amen.

A PRAYER-HEARING GOD

If I put my own good name before the other's highest good, then I know nothing of Calvary love.

—Amy Carmichael

It is the character of the Most High that he is a God who hears prayers.

He sometimes manifests his acceptance of their prayers, by special discoveries of his mercy and sufficiency, which he makes to them *in prayer*, or immediately after. He gives his people special communion with him in prayer. While they are praying, he gives them sweet views of his glorious grace, purity, sufficiency, and sovereignty; and enables them, with great quietness, to rest in him, to leave themselves and their prayers with him, submitting to his will, and trusting in his grace and faithfulness.

Such a manifestation God seems to have made of himself in prayer to *Hannah*. . . . She came and poured out her soul before God, and spake out of the abundance of her complaint and grief; then we read, that she went away, and did eat, and her countenance was no more sad [1 Samuel 1:13], which seems to have been from some refreshing discoveries which God had made of himself to her, to enable her quietly to submit to his will, and trust in his mercy, whereby God manifested his acceptance of her.

—JONATHAN EDWARDS

PRAYER

Thank You, Lord, that You hear every prayer I make, both spoken and unspoken. Amen.

CAST YOUR BURDENS ON THE LORD

How far you go in life depends on your being tender with the young, compassionate with the aged, sympathetic with the striving, and tolerant of the weak and strong. Because someday in life you will have been all of these.

—Attributed to George Washington Carver

Whatsoever it is that presses thee, go tell thy Father; put over the matter into his hand, and so thou shalt be freed from . . . that dividing, perplexing care, that the world is full of. . . .

When thou art either to do or suffer anything, when thou art about any purpose or business, go tell God of it, and acquaint him with it; yea, burden him with it, and thou hast done for matter of caring: no more care, but quiet, sweet diligence in thy duty, and dependence on him for the carriage of thy matters. . . . Roll thy cares, and thyself with them, as one burden all on thy God.

—ROBERT LEIGHTON

PRAYER

Lord, thank You for inviting me to cast my burdens on You. Amen.

THE EYE OF FAITH

Prayer is an act of religion to which there is great encouragement.

—J. C. Ryle

We see that nothing is set before us as an object of expectation from the Lord which we are not enjoined to ask of [him] in prayer, so true it is that prayer digs up those treasures which the Gospel of our Lord discovers to the eye of faith. The necessity and utility of this exercise of prayer no words can sufficiently express. Assuredly it is not without cause our heavenly Father declares that our only safety is in calling upon his name, since by it we invoke the presence of his providence to watch over our interests, of his power to sustain us when weak and almost fainting, of his goodness to receive us into favour, though miserably laded with sin; in fine, call upon him to manifest himself to us in all his perfections. Hence, admirable peace and tranquility are given to our consciences; for the straits by which we were pressed being laid before the Lord, we rest fully satisfied with the assurance that none of our evils are unknown to him, and that he is both able and willing to make the best provision for us.

—JOHN CALVIN

PRAYER

Lord, I pray for peace of mind, knowing that You control all things and see all things. Amen.

MORE VILE

Some people think God does not like to be troubled with our constant coming and asking. The only way to trouble God is not to come at all.

—D. L. Moody

Look that all within you rises higher and higher, by oppositions, threatenings and sufferings, that is, that your faith, your love, your courage, your zeal, your resolutions, and magnanimity rises higher by opposition and a spirit of prayer. Thus it did, Acts 4:18–21, 29–31 compared; all their sufferings did but raise up a more noble spirit in them, they did but raise up their faith and courage. So Acts 5:40–42, they looked on it as a grace to be disgraced for Christ, and as an honour to be dishonoured for him. They say, as David, "If this be to be vile, I will be more vile." If to be found in the way of my God, to act for my God, to be vile, I will be more vile.

—THOMAS BROOKS

PRAYER

Lord, I pray that I speak of You and Your greatness without holding back. May Your words be on my lips. Amen.

LACKING PRAYER

God cannot sustain this free and blessed country, which we love and pray for, unless the church will take right ground.

—Charles Finney

Wherein lay the difficulty with these men? They had been lax in cultivating their faith by prayer and, as a consequence, their trust utterly failed. They trusted not God, nor Christ, nor the authenticity of his mission, or their own. So has it been many a time since, in many a crisis in the church of God. Failure has resulted from a lack of trust, or from a weakness of faith, and this, in turn, from a lack of prayerfulness. Many a failure in revival efforts has been traceable to the same cause. Faith had not been nurtured and made powerful by prayer. Neglect of the inner chamber is the solution of most spiritual failure. And this is as true of our personal struggles with the devil as was the case when we went forth to attempt to cast *out* devils. To be much on our knees in private communion with God is the only surety that we shall have him with us either in our personal struggles, or in our efforts to convert sinners.

—E. M. BOUNDS

PRAYER

Lord, I want to be victorious in my spiritual life, so teach me to spend time on my knees in prayer. Amen.

FAITH IN PRAYER

Each time a man stands up for an ideal, or acts to improve the lot of others, or strikes out against injustice, he sends forth a tiny ripple of hope, and crossing each other from a million different centers of energy and daring those ripples build a current which can sweep down the mightiest walls of oppression and resistance.

—Robert F. Kennedy

What [the man in Luke 11:5–8] has not himself, another can supply. He has a rich friend near, who will be both able and willing to give the bread. He is sure that if he only asks, he will receive. This faith makes him leave his home at midnight: if he has not the bread himself to give, he can ask another.

It is this simple, confident faith that God will give, that we need: where it really exists, there will surely be no mistake about our not praying. In God's Word we have everything that can stir and strengthen such faith in us. Just as the heaven our natural eye can see, is one great ocean of sunshine, with its light and heat, giving beauty and fruitfulness to earth, Scripture shows us God's true heaven, filled with all spiritual blessings, divine light and love and life, heavenly joy and peace and power, all shining down upon us. It reveals to us God waiting, delighting to bestow these blessings in answer to prayer.

—ANDREW MURRAY

PRAYER

If I ask, I will receive. If I seek, I will find. Thank You for hearing and answering my prayer. Amen.

SERVING OTHERS

It is only when you realize your nothingness, your emptiness, that God can fill you with Himself. Souls of prayer are souls of great silence.

—Mother Teresa

In his January 20, 1989, inaugural address, George H. W. Bush gave us this reminder of our actions toward others:

We meet on democracy's front porch, a good place to talk as neighbors and as friends. For this is a day when our nation is made whole, when our differences, for a moment, are suspended.

And my first act as President is a prayer. I ask you to bow your heads:

Heavenly Father, we bow our heads and thank You for Your love. Accept our thanks for the peace that yields this day and the shared faith that makes its continuance likely. Make us strong to do Your work, willing to heed and hear Your will, and write on our hearts these words: "Use power to help people." For we are given power not to advance our own purposes, nor to make a great show in the world, nor a name. There is but one just use of power, and it is to serve people. Help us to remember it, Lord. Amen.

PRAYER

Lord, I pray these words as our president prayed. Use me to help people in our nation now more than ever. Amen.

HOW TO GO TO GOD

The most perfect machinery of government will not keep us as a nation from destruction if there is not within us a soul. No abounding material prosperity shall avail us if our spiritual senses atrophy.

—Theodore Roosevelt

There must be a hearty renunciation of everything that does not lead us to God and a continual conversation with Him, with freedom and in simplicity. We will recognize that God is intimately present with us, importuning us to address ourselves to Him, that we may beg His assistance for knowing His will in things doubtful, and for rightfully performing those which we plainly see He requires of us. . . .

In this conversation with God, we are also employed in praising, adoring, and loving Him incessantly for His infinite goodness and perfection. . . .

It is a great delusion to think that the times of prayer ought differ from other times. It is also a great delusion to believe that we are as strictly obliged to adhere to God by action in the time of action, as by prayer in its season.

—ADAPTED FROM BROTHER LAWRENCE

PRAYER

Lord, teach me that prayer is an ongoing conversation with You, all day long. Amen.

PRAYER IS LIFE

Both [North and South] read the same Bible, and pray to the same God; and each invokes His aid against the other.

It may seem strange that any men should dare to ask a just God's assistance in wringing their bread from the sweat of other men's faces; but let us judge not that we be not judged. The prayers of both could not be answered; that of neither has been answered fully. The Almighty has His own purposes.

—Abraham Lincoln

Prayer is the heart of Christian life. It is essential. Prayer is both the first step and the fulfillment of the devout life. We are directed to pray always. Particular times may be set for other acts of devotion, but for prayer there is no special time. We are to pray constantly.

Sit alone in a quiet place. Take your mind away from every earthly and vain thing. Bow your head to your chest and be attentive, not to your head, but to your heart. Observe your breathing. Let your mind find the place of the heart. At first you will be uncomfortable. If you continue without interruption, it will become a joy.

—ANONYMOUS

PRAYER

Lord, I trust in You and ask for Your guidance and wisdom to make the right choices. Amen.

THERE'S HOPE IN SILENCE

A simple, childlike faith in a Divine Friend solves all the problems that come to us by land or sea.

—Helen Keller

Imagine a soul so closely united to God that it has no need of outward acts to remain attentive to the inward prayer. In these moments of silence and peace when it pays no heed to what is happening within itself, it prays and prays excellently, with a simple and direct prayer that God will understand perfectly by the action of grace.

The heart will be full of aspirations toward God without any clear expression. If it is the heart that prays, it is evident that sometimes and even continuously, it can pray by itself without any help from words, spoken or not. Here is something that few people understand. Though prayers may elude our own consciousness, they will not escape the consciousness of God.

This prayer, so empty of all images and perceptions, apparently so passive and yet so active, is—so far as the limitations of this life allow—pure adoration in spirit and in truth. . . . This is what is called the prayer of silent or of quiet or of bare faith.

—ADAPTED FROM JEAN NICOLAS GROU

PRAYER

Father, teach me to be still and wait on You. Amen.

THE GRACIOUS HAND

We tend to use prayer as a last resort, but God wants it to be our first line of defense.

—Oswald Chambers

In deep concern over the devastation of civil war, President Abraham Lincoln declared a National Fast Day on March 30, 1863:

We have been the recipients of the choicest bounties of Heaven; we have been preserved these many years in peace and prosperity; we have grown in numbers, wealth, and power as no other nation has ever grown. But we have forgotten God. We have forgotten the gracious hand which preserved us in peace and multiplied and enriched and strengthened us, and we have vainly imagined, in the deceitfulness of our hearts, that all these blessings were produced by some superior wisdom and virtue of our own. Intoxicated with unbroken success, we have become too self-sufficient to feel the necessity of redeeming and preserving grace, too proud to pray to the God that made us.

It behooves us, then, to humble ourselves before the offended Power, to confess our national sins, and to pray for clemency and forgiveness.

PRAYER

Lord, may the words I speak to You in prayer be meaningful and effective. Amen.

SHIFTING GEARS

You can do what you have to do, and sometimes you can do it even better than you think you can.

—As quoted by Jimmy Carter

After a time of meditation, immediately begin to put into practice the resolutions you have made. Don't wait another day to get started. Without this application, meditation may be useless or even detrimental. Meditate on a virtue without practicing it, and you will mislead yourself into believing that you have actually become someone you are not. . . .

When your silent prayer is over, remain still and quiet for a few moments. Make your transition to other responsibilities gradually. Linger yet a while in the garden. Walk carefully along the path through the gate so that you won't spill the precious balm you are carrying. Don't be unnatural around other people, but keep as much prayer in you as you can.

There is an art to making the transition from prayer to earning a living. A lawyer must go from prayer to the courtroom, the merchant to the store, a homemaker to appointed responsibilities with a gentle motion that will not cause distress. Both prayer and your other duties are gifts from God.

—ADAPTED FROM SAINT FRANCIS DE SALES

PRAYER

O Lord, I simply ask that my work and my prayer life will benefit others. Amen.

PRAYER MAKES A DIFFERENCE

When you have read the Bible you will know it is the Word of God, because you will have found it the key to your own heart, your own happiness, and your duty.

—Woodrow Wilson

In Christ we have continual peace under all trials, and through him we have power in prayer to obtain from the Lord all things necessary for this life and godliness. It has been the writer's lot to test the Lord hundreds of times about temporal needs, being driven thereto by the care of orphans and students. Prayer has many, many times brought opportune supplies and cleared away serious difficulties. I know that faith can fill a purse, provide a meal, change a hard heart, procure a site for a building, heal sickness, quiet insubordination, and stay an epidemic. Like money in the worldling's hand, faith in the hand of the man of God "answereth all things." All things in heaven, and earth, and under the earth, answer to the command of prayer. . . . How I wish that my reader would so believe in God as to lean upon him in all the concerns of his life!

—CHARLES SPURGEON

PRAYER

Father God, thank You for the simple, beautiful truth that You hear my prayers. Amen.

PRAYER BRINGS REVIVAL

When a long train of abuses and usurpations, pursuing invariably the same object, evinces a design to reduce them under absolute despotism, it is their duty to throw off such government, and to provide new guards for their future security. Such has been the patient sufferance of women under this government, and such is now the necessity which constrains them to demand the equal station to which they are entitled.

—Elizabeth Cady Stanton

[This revival] will be fulfilled after this manner: There shall be given much of a spirit of prayer to God's people, in many places, disposing them to come into an express *agreement,* unitedly to pray to God in an extraordinary manner, that he would appear for the help of his church, and in mercy to mankind, and *pour out his Spirit, revive his work*, and advance his spiritual *kingdom* in the world, as he has promised. This disposition to prayer, and union in it, will gradually spread more and more, and increase to greater degrees; with which at length will gradually be introduced *a revival of religion.*

. . . The manner of prayer agreed on is literally, "Let us go in going." . . . When it is said in the text, "Let us go in going, and pray before the Lord," the strength of the expression represents the *earnestness* of those that make the proposal . . . that they should be *speedy, fervent*, and *constant* in it; or, in one word, that it should be *thoroughly* performed. . . .

—JONATHAN EDWARDS

PRAYER

Father, break forth a revival in our nation and in the world. Bring Your revival to pass. Amen.

THE FATHER OF LIGHTS

We must not forget that we take these gifts upon the condition that justice and mercy shall hold the reins of power and that the upward avenues of hope shall be free to all the people.

—Benjamin Harrison

After the British surrender, the American colonies had a nation but sought a framework to govern it. In May 1787, delegates gathered in Philadelphia to draft a constitution that would establish a strong and effective federal government. However, the delegates quickly found themselves divided over what this new government should look like and how much power it should wield.

Amid these heated debates, Benjamin Franklin, known for his intellect and not necessarily for his faith, rose to address the room. At eighty-one years old, Franklin urged his fellow delegates to acknowledge the sovereignty and guidance of heaven. He proposed that each session begin with daily prayer, firmly believing that wisdom, unity, and clarity in their mission could only come through seeking the will of God.

Franklin's call to prayer was a poignant reminder to the delegates of the spiritual foundation necessary to guide their efforts and encouraged a sense of humility as they worked to shape the future of the fledgling nation.

PRAYER

Lord, I humbly ask that You draw our nation back to faithful obedience to You. Amen.

KEEPING PRAYER FOCUSED

Had the doctrines of Jesus been preached always as purely as they came from his lips, the whole civilised world would now have been Christian.

—Thomas Jefferson

Nothing is more essential for the Christian, or more neglected, than prayer. Most people are not excited about praying. They find it a tiring ritual that they like to keep as short as possible. Even when we are led to prayer by responsibilities or anxieties, our prayers are often dull and ineffective.

Many words are unnecessary. To pray is to say, "Not my will, but thine, be done" (Luke 22:42). To pray is to lift up your heart to God, to be sorry for your weakness, to regret your constant stumbling. Prayer of this kind requires no special formula. You don't even have to stop doing whatever it is that is keeping you busy. All that is needed is a movement of the heart toward God and a desire that what you are doing may be done for his glory.

—ADAPTED FROM FRANÇOIS FÉNELON

PRAYER

Lord, give this nation what we don't know how to request from You. Amen.

DOING GOOD

The name of Jesus is a never-failing passport for our prayers. In that name a person may draw near to God with boldness, and ask with confidence. God has engaged to hear him.

—J. C. Ryle

Be always doing or receiving good. Our Lord and Master went up and down in this world doing good; he was still doing good to body and soul; he was acted by an untired power. Be still doing or receiving good. This will make your lives comfortable, your deaths happy, and your account glorious, in the great day of our Lord. Oh! how useless are many men in their generation! Oh! that our lips might be as so many honey-combs, that we might scatter knowledge!

—THOMAS BROOKS

PRAYER

Lord, may my life be about doing Your work and Your work alone! Amen.

THE FATHER'S POWERFUL LOVE

Prayer is a sincere, sensible, affectionate pouring out of the soul to God, through Christ, in the power of the Holy Spirit, for such things as He has promised, for the good of the church with submission in faith to the will of God.

—John Bunyan

We have often walked in the fields in the early morning, and have noticed how the rising sun has turned each dewdrop into a glittering gem: one ray of its own bright light making a little sun of each of the million drops that hang from the pendent leaflets and sparkle everywhere. But it is helpful to remember that the glorious orb itself contains infinitely more light than all the dewdrops ever did or ever will reflect. And so of our Heavenly Father: Himself the great Source of all that is noble and true, of all that ever has been loving and trustworthy—each beautiful trait of each beautiful character is but the dim reflection of some ray of His own great perfection. And the sum-total of all human goodness and tenderness, and love is but as the dewdrops to the sun. How blessed then to confide in the infinite and changeless love of such a Father—*our Father in Heaven.*

—HUDSON TAYLOR

PRAYER

Father, I worship You for all the wonder that You are. Amen.

GEORGE WASHINGTON'S FAREWELL ADDRESS

September 17, 1796

As his second term ended, George Washington announced his retirement in a letter to the American people. Although many feared for the country's future without him, he reassured the nation of its readiness. Washington advised on national prosperity and warned against political parties, factions, and animosities that could undermine the government:

This spirit [of party], unfortunately, is inseparable from our nature, having its root in the strongest passions of the human mind. . . .

The disorders and miseries which result gradually incline the minds of men to seek security and repose in the absolute power of an individual; and sooner or later the chief of some prevailing faction, more able or more fortunate than his competitors, turns this disposition to the purposes of his own elevation, on the ruins of public liberty.

Without looking forward to an extremity of this kind (which nevertheless ought not to be entirely out of sight), the common and continual mischiefs of the spirit of party are sufficient to make it the interest and duty of a wise people to discourage and restrain it. . . .

A fire not to be quenched, it demands a uniform vigilance to prevent its bursting into a flame, lest, instead of warming, it should consume.

PRAYER

Lord, help me always to consider others more important than myself. Amen.

THE HABIT OF PRAYER

Die when I may I want it said of me by those who know me best to say that I always plucked a thistle and planted a flower where I thought a flower would grow.

—Abraham Lincoln

O my brother! if thou and I would be like Jesus, we must especially contemplate Jesus praying alone in the wilderness. There is the secret of His wonderful life. What He did and spoke to man, was first Spoken and lived through with the Father. In communion with Him, the anointing with the Holy Spirit was each day renewed. He who would be like Him in his walk and conversation, must simply begin here, that he follows Jesus into solitude. . . . Besides the ordinary hour of prayer, he will feel at times irresistibly drawn to enter into the holy place, and not to come thence until it has anew been revealed to him that God is his portion. In his secret chamber, with closed door, or in the solitude of the wilderness, God must be found every day, and our fellowship with Him renewed. If Christ needed it, how much more we! What it was to Him it will be for us.

—ANDREW MURRAY

PRAYER

Father, give me the discipline I need to spend time in the secret chamber of prayer with You each day. Amen.

LOVE AND ANSWERED PRAYERS

Authority without wisdom is like a heavy axe without an edge—fitter to bruise than polish.

—Anne Bradstreet

Almighty God is the very highest model, and to be like Him is to possess the highest character. Prayer moulds us into the image of God, and at the same time tends to mould others into the same image just in proportion as we pray for others. Prayer means to be God-like, and to be God-like is to love Christ and love God, to be one with the Father and the Son in spirit, character and conduct. . . .

God has much to do with believing [people], who have a living, transforming faith in Jesus Christ. These are God's children. A father loves his children, supplies their needs, hears their cries, and answers their requests. A child believes his father, loves him, trusts in him, and asks him for what he needs, believing without doubting that his father will hear his requests. God has everything to do with answering the prayer of His children. Their troubles concern Him, and their prayers awaken Him. Their voice is sweet to Him. He loves to hear them pray, and He is never happier than to answer their prayers.

—E. M. BOUNDS

PRAYER

Heavenly Father, I thank You that You love to hear and answer my prayers to You! Amen.

PRAYER FROM THE HEART

To pray rightly, you must make God your hope, stay, and all. Right prayer sees nothing substantial or worth being concerned about except God.

—John Bunyan

God," says Jesus Christ, "is a Spirit, and they that adore him, must adore him in spirit and in truth" [John 4:24]. Prayer therefore is wholly a spiritual act, directed to Him who is the Spirit of spirits, the Spirit who sees all things and who is, as St. Augustine says, more intimately present to our soul than its deepest depths. If we add to what is of the essence of prayer certain bodily postures, words, external marks of devotion; all these of themselves mean nothing, and are only pleasing to God inasmuch as they express the sentiments of the soul. It is, speaking properly, the *heart* that prays; it is to the voice of the heart that God lends an attentive ear. Whoever speaks of the heart means that which is most spiritual within us.

—JEAN NICOLAS GROU

PRAYER

Father, I seek You with my whole heart, and I know that You hear me when I pray. Amen.

A SINCERE PERSON

To pray, my brethren, is to cast off your burdens, it is to tear away your rags, it is to shake off your diseases, it is to be filled with spiritual vigour, it is to reach the highest point of Christian health.

—Charles Spurgeon

Love gives the character to a man, according as the object is which he superlatively loved. As is the love—such is the man. As is the love—such might you boldly call the man. If he is a lover of honor—then he is an ambitious man. If he is a lover of pleasure—then he is a voluptuous man. If he chiefly loves the world—then he is a covetous man. If he loves holiness—then he is a pious man. If he loves the things above—then he is a heavenly-minded man. If he loves Christ with a supreme love—then he is a Christian man!

—ADAPTED FROM THOMAS DOOLITTLE

PRAYER

Lord, may others look at me and this country, seeing Your hand upon us. Amen.

PRAYING TO A GOOD GOD

If you would'st live long, live well; for Folly and Wickedness shorten Life.

—Benjamin Franklin

So needful is prayer to the soul that the mere attitude of it may encourage a good mood. Verily to pray to that which is not, is in logic a folly; yet the good that, they say, comes of it, may rebuke the worse folly of their unbelief, for it indicates that prayer is natural, and how could it be natural if inconsistent with the very mode of our being? Theirs is a better way than that of those who, believing there is a God, but not believing that he will give any answer to their prayers, yet pray to him; that is more foolish and more immoral than praying to the No-god. Whatever the God be to whom they pray, their prayer is a mockery of him, of themselves, of the truth.

—GEORGE MACDONALD

PRAYER

Thank You, Father, for the privilege of prayer and for the opportunity to have a relationship with You. Amen.

THE SHADOW WARRIORS: THE CULPER SPY RING

Their humility stopped them from seeking fame or fortune because their love of country sparked their exploits.

—George Washington

During the Revolution, as soldiers clashed, another war unfolded in the shadows. In 1778, the British held New York City and intelligence was scarce. To gain an edge, George Washington enlisted the Culper Spy Ring—patriots risking everything for freedom.

In secrecy, ordinary citizens became heroes. Abraham Woodhull and Robert Townsend used aliases, disguises, and codes to track British troop movements, supply lines, and plans. They sent messages across rivers using dead drops and invisible ink under British officers' noses. Each faced life-and-death consequences.

Their work was perilous. If caught, they faced execution. Yet they delivered information that helped Washington decide what to do next. Loyalists and British spies never suspected that farmers, shopkeepers, and tavern owners shaped the war behind the scenes.

The Culper Spy Ring showed that battles depend on more than muskets. These secret warriors, with cunning and bravery, kept hope alive from the shadows. Their legacy reveals that courage takes many forms and victory is often silent.

PRAYER

Lord, please help me not to be silent when I see others hurting. Give me the courage to speak up and serve You. Amen.

NURTURING PRAYER

The true republic—men, their rights and nothing more; women, their rights and nothing less.

—Susan B. Anthony

The proper thing is for us always to think of God and pray without ceasing. If we are not able to achieve this, we can at least set special times for prayer each day. At these designated moments we can focus entirely on God. . . .

This is only a start, of course. We should not think of these times of prayer as a ritual. Neither do they mean we are freed from prayer at other hours of the day. Think of these moments as nothing more than a discipline for your spiritual weakness. It is a stimulation for your groggy soul. There will be times when you are under stress, times when you will be aware of others in difficulty. Immediately turn to God in prayer. Offer prayers of thanks all through the day.

When you pray, do not put any limits on God. It is not your business to tell God how to answer your prayers. This is not a time to bargain or to set conditions. Before you tell God what you want or need, ask that his will may be done. This makes your will subordinate to his.

—ADAPTED FROM JOHN CALVIN

PRAYER

Lord, thank You for hearing every prayer I make, no matter how small or simple. Amen.

PRAYING FOR MERCY

To the influence of this Book [the Bible] we are indebted for all the progress made in true civilization, and to this we must look for our guide in the future.

—Ulysses S. Grant

The Scripture does not only abundantly manifest it to be the duty of God's people to be much in prayer for this great mercy, but it also abounds with manifold considerations to *encourage* them in it, and animate them with hopes of *success*. There is perhaps no one thing that the Bible so much promises, in order to encourage the faith, hope, and prayers of the saints, as this; which affords God's people the clearest evidences that it is their *duty* to be much in prayer for this mercy. For, undoubtedly, that which God abundantly makes the subject of his promises, God's people should abundantly make the subject of their *prayers*. It also affords them the strongest assurances that their prayers shall be *successful*. With what confidence may we go before God, and pray for that, of which we have so many exceeding precious and glorious promises to plead!

—JONATHAN EDWARDS

PRAYER

O Lord, pour out Your Spirit in my life, and let me experience You in a fresh, new way. Amen.

BLESSED TO BE A BLESSING

You have not lived today until you have done something for someone who can never repay you.

—John Bunyan

Here is a question for the rich. How is it that you happen to be rich? Is it because God has blessed you? By what means did you receive this blessing? Is it through prayer? You prayed for riches and God gave you riches? Very well.

But answer another question. What do others, who are not rich, seek in prayer? Do they not pray the same way you do? If everyone prays for riches then it must be that your riches are not the result of your own prayers only, but also of others who have helped you pray. . . . It follows that since you did not receive your riches through your own prayers alone, but through the prayers of the poor, then you are obligated to relieve poverty in any way you can.

. . . Why does God give some a hundred and another thousands and some nothing at all? Here is the meaning. The rich are to distribute riches among the poor. Those who are rich are God's officers, God's treasurers.

—ADAPTED FROM HUGH LATIMER

PRAYER

Lord, let me be Your treasurer and share in Your name. Amen.

TWO OBSTACLES TO PRAYER

In every human Breast, God has implanted a Principle, which we call Love of Freedom.

—Phillis Wheatley

There are two major obstacles to prayer. The first obstacle arises when the devil prompts you to think, "I am not yet prepared to pray. I should wait for another half-hour or another day until I have become more prepared or until I have finished taking care of this or that." Meanwhile, the devil distracts you for half an hour, so that you no longer think about prayer for the rest of the day; from one day to the next, you are hindered and rushed with other business. This common obstacle shows us how maliciously the devil tries to trick us. . . .

The second obstacle arises when we ask ourselves, "How can you pray to God and say the Lord's Prayer? You are too unworthy and sin every day. Wait until you are more devout." This serious obstacle crushes us like a heavy stone. Despite our feelings of unworthiness, our hearts must struggle to remove this obstacle so that we can freely approach God and call upon him.

—ADAPTED FROM MARTIN LUTHER

PRAYER

Heavenly Father, keep me from distractions and feelings of unworthiness as I come to You in prayer. Amen.

PERSONAL RESPONSIBILITY FOR THE LOST

The Declaration of Independence is the ringbolt to the chain of your nation's destiny; so, indeed, I regard it. The principles contained in that instrument are saving principles. Stand by those principles, be true to them on all occasions, in all places, against all foes, and at whatever cost.

—Frederick Douglass

Each servant of God must have love for souls—the kind of love that God had in giving up His Son to die, and that Christ had in coming down cheerfully to make Himself the offering—or his prayers for this purpose will have little heart and no power with God. This love for souls is always implied in acceptable prayer—prayer that God would send forth laborers into His harvest. I have often thought that the reason why so many pray only in form and not in heart for the salvation of souls is that they lack this love—the love of God—for the souls of the perishing. . . .

You must see that souls are precious. . . . Without such a sense of the value of the interests at stake, you will not pray with fervent, strong desire; and without a proper understanding of their guilt, danger, and remedy, you will not pray in faith for God's intervening grace.

—CHARLES FINNEY

PRAYER

Lord Jesus, give me a heart for lost people in our nation and the world. Amen.

SILENT PRAYER

What God says is best, is best, though all the men in the world are against it.

—John Bunyan

Start every prayer in the presence of God. Be strict about this and you will soon see its value. Don't rush through your prayers. The Lord's Prayer said once with comprehension is better than many prayers said in haste.

If you can do it, inward, silent prayer is best. If you are reciting a standard prayer and find your heart being drawn deeper, by all means leave the spoken prayer behind and move into silence. Don't worry about leaving your formal prayer unfinished. Your silent prayer pleases God the most, and it will be better for your soul.

Be diligent about this. Don't let a morning pass without some time in silent prayer. But if the demands of business or some other responsibility prevents it, then be sure to repair the damage that evening. Make a vow to start your regular practice of morning prayer again tomorrow.

—ADAPTED FROM SAINT FRANCIS DE SALES

PRAYER

Dear Lord, let my daily inner prayers take on a vibrant life. Amen.

A PATH FORGED TO DEMOCRACY

We the People of the United States, in Order to form a more perfect Union, establish Justice, insure domestic Tranquility, provide for the common defence, promote the general Welfare, and secure the Blessings of Liberty to ourselves and our Posterity, do ordain and establish this Constitution for the United States of America.

—Preamble, United States Constitution

In 1787, delegates from several states gathered in Philadelphia, burdened by a weak nation. The Articles of Confederation had left the United States unable to manage debts, enforce laws, or defend its borders. In the summer heat, leaders like George Washington, James Madison, and Benjamin Franklin met at Independence Hall to forge a new path.

Debates were intense. Madison and allies argued for a system of checks and balances, with three branches—legislative, executive, judicial—each able to limit the others, preventing dominance.

The Constitution split power between the federal government and states, creating shared authority. Delegates debated representation, taxation, defense, and law, knowing the nation's survival was at stake.

When the Constitution was signed on September 17, 1787, it became a promise: Government would serve the people; liberty and order could coexist; the United States could grow from fragile colonies to a lasting republic.

PRAYER

Lord, thank You for giving our nation leaders who loved and listened to You during the building of America. Amen.

UNITED STATES CONSTITUTION

We the People of the United States, in Order to form a more perfect Union, establish Justice, insure domestic Tranquility, provide for the common defence, promote the general Welfare, and secure the Blessings of Liberty to ourselves and our Posterity, do ordain and establish this Constitution for the United States of America.

ARTICLE. I.

Section. 1.

All legislative Powers herein granted shall be vested in a Congress of the United States, which shall consist of a Senate and House of Representatives.

Section. 2.

The House of Representatives shall be composed of Members chosen every second Year by the People of the several States, and the Electors in each State shall have the Qualifications requisite for Electors of the most numerous Branch of the State Legislature.

No Person shall be a Representative who shall not have attained to the Age of twenty five Years, and been seven Years a Citizen of the United States, and who shall not, when elected, be an Inhabitant of that State in which he shall be chosen.

Representatives and direct Taxes shall be apportioned among the several States which may be included within this Union, according to their respective Numbers, which shall be determined by adding to the whole Number of free Persons, including those bound to Service for a Term of Years, and excluding Indians not taxed, three fifths of all other Persons. The actual Enumeration shall be made within three Years after the first Meeting of the Congress of the

United States, and within every subsequent Term of ten Years, in such Manner as they shall by Law direct. The Number of Representatives shall not exceed one for every thirty Thousand, but each State shall have at Least one Representative; and until such enumeration shall be made, the State of New Hampshire shall be entitled to chuse three, Massachusetts eight, Rhode-Island and Providence Plantations one, Connecticut five, New-York six, New Jersey four, Pennsylvania eight, Delaware one, Maryland six, Virginia ten, North Carolina five, South Carolina five, and Georgia three.

When vacancies happen in the Representation from any State, the Executive Authority thereof shall issue Writs of Election to fill such Vacancies.

The House of Representatives shall chuse their Speaker and other Officers; and shall have the sole Power of Impeachment.

Section. 3.

The Senate of the United States shall be composed of two Senators from each State, chosen by the Legislature thereof, for six Years; and each Senator shall have one Vote.

Immediately after they shall be assembled in Consequence of the first Election, they shall be divided as equally as may be into three Classes. The Seats of the Senators of the first Class shall be vacated at the Expiration of the second Year, of the second Class at the Expiration of the fourth Year, and of the third Class at the Expiration of the sixth Year, so that one third may be chosen every second Year; and if Vacancies happen by Resignation, or otherwise, during the Recess of the Legislature of any State, the Executive thereof may make temporary Appointments until the next Meeting of the Legislature, which shall then fill such Vacancies.

No Person shall be a Senator who shall not have attained to the Age of thirty Years, and been nine Years a Citizen of the United States, and who shall not, when elected, be an Inhabitant of that State for which he shall be chosen.

The Vice President of the United States shall be President of the Senate, but shall have no Vote, unless they be equally divided.

The Senate shall chuse their other Officers, and also a President pro tempore, in the Absence of the Vice President, or when he shall exercise the Office of President of the United States.

The Senate shall have the sole Power to try all Impeachments. When sitting for that Purpose, they shall be on Oath or Affirmation. When the President of the United States is tried, the Chief Justice shall preside: And no Person shall be convicted without the Concurrence of two thirds of the Members present.

Judgment in Cases of Impeachment shall not extend further than to removal from Office, and disqualification to hold and enjoy any Office of honor, Trust or Profit under the United States: but the Party convicted shall nevertheless be liable and subject to Indictment, Trial, Judgment and Punishment, according to Law.

Section. 4.

The Times, Places and Manner of holding Elections for Senators and Representatives, shall be prescribed in each State by the Legislature thereof; but the Congress may at any time by Law make or alter such Regulations, except as to the Places of chusing Senators.

The Congress shall assemble at least once in every Year, and such Meeting shall be on the first Monday in December, unless they shall by Law appoint a different Day.

Section. 5.

Each House shall be the Judge of the Elections, Returns and Qualifications of its own Members, and a Majority of each shall constitute a Quorum to do Business; but a smaller Number may adjourn from day to day, and may be authorized to compel the Attendance of absent Members, in such Manner, and under such Penalties as each House may provide.

Each House may determine the Rules of its Proceedings, punish its Members for disorderly Behaviour, and, with the Concurrence of two thirds, expel a Member.

Each House shall keep a Journal of its Proceedings, and from time to time publish the same, excepting such Parts as may in their Judgment require Secrecy; and the Yeas and Nays of the Members of either House on any question shall, at the Desire of one fifth of those Present, be entered on the Journal.

Neither House, during the Session of Congress, shall, without the Consent of the other, adjourn for more than three days, nor to any other Place than that in which the two Houses shall be sitting.

Section. 6.

The Senators and Representatives shall receive a Compensation for their Services, to be ascertained by Law, and paid out of the Treasury of the United States. They shall in all Cases, except Treason, Felony and Breach of the Peace, be privileged from Arrest during their Attendance at the Session of their respective Houses, and in going to and returning from the same; and for any Speech or Debate in either House, they shall not be questioned in any other Place.

No Senator or Representative shall, during the Time for which he was elected, be appointed to any civil Office under the Authority of the United States, which shall have been created, or the Emoluments whereof shall have been encreased during such time; and no Person holding any Office under the United States, shall be a Member of either House during his Continuance in Office.

Section. 7.

All Bills for raising Revenue shall originate in the House of Representatives; but the Senate may propose or concur with Amendments as on other Bills.

Every Bill which shall have passed the House of Representatives and the Senate, shall, before it become a Law, be presented to the President of the United States; If he approve he shall sign it, but if not he shall return it, with his Objections to that House in which it shall have originated, who shall enter the Objections at large on their Journal, and proceed to reconsider it. If after such Reconsideration two thirds of that House shall agree to pass the Bill, it shall be sent, together with the Objections, to the other House, by which it shall likewise be reconsidered, and if approved by two thirds of that House, it shall become a Law. But in all such Cases the Votes of both Houses shall be determined by yeas and Nays, and the Names of the Persons voting for and against the Bill shall be entered on the Journal of each House respectively. If any Bill shall not be returned by the President within ten Days (Sundays excepted) after it shall have been presented to him, the Same shall be a Law, in like Manner as if he had signed it, unless the Congress by their Adjournment prevent its Return, in which Case it shall not be a Law.

Every Order, Resolution, or Vote to which the Concurrence of the Senate and House of Representatives may be necessary (except on a question of

Adjournment) shall be presented to the President of the United States; and before the Same shall take Effect, shall be approved by him, or being disapproved by him, shall be repassed by two thirds of the Senate and House of Representatives, according to the Rules and Limitations prescribed in the Case of a Bill.

Section. 8.

The Congress shall have Power To lay and collect Taxes, Duties, Imposts and Excises, to pay the Debts and provide for the common Defence and general Welfare of the United States; but all Duties, Imposts and Excises shall be uniform throughout the United States;

To borrow Money on the credit of the United States;

To regulate Commerce with foreign Nations, and among the several States, and with the Indian Tribes;

To establish an uniform Rule of Naturalization, and uniform Laws on the subject of Bankruptcies throughout the United States;

To coin Money, regulate the Value thereof, and of foreign Coin, and fix the Standard of Weights and Measures;

To provide for the Punishment of counterfeiting the Securities and current Coin of the United States;

To establish Post Offices and post Roads;

To promote the Progress of Science and useful Arts, by securing for limited Times to Authors and Inventors the exclusive Right to their respective Writings and Discoveries;

To constitute Tribunals inferior to the supreme Court;

To define and punish Piracies and Felonies committed on the high Seas, and Offences against the Law of Nations;

To declare War, grant Letters of Marque and Reprisal, and make Rules concerning Captures on Land and Water;

To raise and support Armies, but no Appropriation of Money to that Use shall be for a longer Term than two Years;

To provide and maintain a Navy;

To make Rules for the Government and Regulation of the land and naval Forces;

To provide for calling forth the Militia to execute the Laws of the Union, suppress Insurrections and repel Invasions;

To provide for organizing, arming, and disciplining, the Militia, and for governing such Part of them as may be employed in the Service of the United States, reserving to the States respectively, the Appointment of the Officers, and the Authority of training the Militia according to the discipline prescribed by Congress;

To exercise exclusive Legislation in all Cases whatsoever, over such District (not exceeding ten Miles square) as may, by Cession of particular States, and the Acceptance of Congress, become the Seat of the Government of the United States, and to exercise like Authority over all Places purchased by the Consent of the Legislature of the State in which the Same shall be, for the Erection of Forts, Magazines, Arsenals, dock-Yards, and other needful Buildings;—And

To make all Laws which shall be necessary and proper for carrying into Execution the foregoing Powers, and all other Powers vested by this Constitution in the Government of the United States, or in any Department or Officer thereof.

Section. 9.

The Migration or Importation of such Persons as any of the States now existing shall think proper to admit, shall not be prohibited by the Congress prior to the Year one thousand eight hundred and eight, but a Tax or duty may be imposed on such Importation, not exceeding ten dollars for each Person.

The Privilege of the Writ of Habeas Corpus shall not be suspended, unless when in Cases of Rebellion or Invasion the public Safety may require it.

No Bill of Attainder or ex post facto Law shall be passed.

No Capitation, or other direct, Tax shall be laid, unless in Proportion to the Census or enumeration herein before directed to be taken.

No Tax or Duty shall be laid on Articles exported from any State.

No Preference shall be given by any Regulation of Commerce or Revenue to the Ports of one State over those of another: nor shall Vessels bound to, or from, one State, be obliged to enter, clear, or pay Duties in another.

No Money shall be drawn from the Treasury, but in Consequence of Appropriations made by Law; and a regular Statement and Account of the Receipts and Expenditures of all public Money shall be published from time to time.

No Title of Nobility shall be granted by the United States: And no Person holding any Office of Profit or Trust under them, shall, without the Consent of the Congress, accept of any present, Emolument, Office, or Title, of any kind whatever, from any King, Prince, or foreign State.

Section. 10.

No State shall enter into any Treaty, Alliance, or Confederation; grant Letters of Marque and Reprisal; coin Money; emit Bills of Credit; make any Thing but gold and silver Coin a Tender in Payment of Debts; pass any Bill of Attainder, ex post facto Law, or Law impairing the Obligation of Contracts, or grant any Title of Nobility.

No State shall, without the Consent of the Congress, lay any Imposts or Duties on Imports or Exports, except what may be absolutely necessary for executing it's inspection Laws: and the net Produce of all Duties and Imposts, laid by any State on Imports or Exports, shall be for the Use of the Treasury of the United States; and all such Laws shall be subject to the Revision and Controul of the Congress.

No State shall, without the Consent of Congress, lay any Duty of Tonnage, keep Troops, or Ships of War in time of Peace, enter into any Agreement or Compact with another State, or with a foreign Power, or engage in War, unless actually invaded, or in such imminent Danger as will not admit of delay.

ARTICLE. II.

Section. 1.

The executive Power shall be vested in a President of the United States of America. He shall hold his Office during the Term of four Years, and, together with the Vice President, chosen for the same Term, be elected, as follows

Each State shall appoint, in such Manner as the Legislature thereof may direct, a Number of Electors, equal to the whole Number of Senators and Representatives to which the State may be entitled in the Congress: but no Senator or Representative, or Person holding an Office of Trust or Profit under the United States, shall be appointed an Elector.

The Electors shall meet in their respective States, and vote by Ballot for two Persons, of whom one at least shall not be an Inhabitant of the same State with themselves. And they shall make a List of all the Persons voted for, and of the Number of Votes for each; which List they shall sign and certify, and transmit sealed to the Seat of the Government of the United States, directed to the President of the Senate. The President of the Senate shall, in the Presence of the Senate and House of Representatives, open all the Certificates, and the Votes shall then be counted. The Person having the greatest Number of Votes shall be the President, if such Number be a Majority of the whole Number of Electors appointed; and if there be more than one who have such Majority, and have an equal Number of Votes, then the House of Representatives shall immediately chuse by Ballot one of them for President; and if no Person have a Majority, then from the five highest on the List the said House shall in like Manner chuse the President. But in chusing the President, the Votes shall be taken by States, the Representation from each State having one Vote; A quorum for this Purpose shall consist of a Member or Members from two thirds of the States, and a Majority of all the States shall be necessary to a Choice. In every Case, after the Choice of the President, the Person having the greatest Number of Votes of the Electors shall be the Vice President. But if there should remain two or more who have equal Votes, the Senate shall chuse from them by Ballot the Vice President.

The Congress may determine the Time of chusing the Electors, and the Day on which they shall give their Votes; which Day shall be the same throughout the United States.

No Person except a natural born Citizen, or a Citizen of the United States, at the time of the Adoption of this Constitution, shall be eligible to the Office of President; neither shall any Person be eligible to that Office who shall not have attained to the Age of thirty five Years, and been fourteen Years a Resident within the United States.

In Case of the Removal of the President from Office, or of his Death, Resignation, or Inability to discharge the Powers and Duties of the said Office, the Same shall devolve on the Vice President, and the Congress may by Law provide for the Case of Removal, Death, Resignation or Inability, both of the President and Vice President, declaring what Officer shall then act as President, and such Officer shall act accordingly, until the Disability be removed, or a President shall be elected.

The President shall, at stated Times, receive for his Services, a Compensation, which shall neither be encreased nor diminished during the Period for which he shall have been elected, and he shall not receive within that Period any other Emolument from the United States, or any of them.

Before he enter on the Execution of his Office, he shall take the following Oath or Affirmation:—"I do solemnly swear (or affirm) that I will faithfully execute the Office of President of the United States, and will to the best of my Ability, preserve, protect and defend the Constitution of the United States."

Section. 2.

The President shall be Commander in Chief of the Army and Navy of the United States, and of the Militia of the several States, when called into the actual Service of the United States; he may require the Opinion, in writing, of the principal Officer in each of the executive Departments, upon any Subject relating to the Duties of their respective Offices, and he shall have Power to grant Reprieves and Pardons for Offences against the United States, except in Cases of Impeachment.

He shall have Power, by and with the Advice and Consent of the Senate, to make Treaties, provided two thirds of the Senators present concur; and he shall nominate, and by and with the Advice and Consent of the Senate, shall appoint Ambassadors, other public Ministers and Consuls, Judges of the supreme Court, and all other Officers of the United States, whose Appointments are not herein otherwise provided for, and which shall be established by Law: but the Congress may by Law vest the Appointment of such inferior Officers, as they think proper, in the President alone, in the Courts of Law, or in the Heads of Departments.

The President shall have Power to fill up all Vacancies that may happen during the Recess of the Senate, by granting Commissions which shall expire at the End of their next Session.

Section. 3.

He shall from time to time give to the Congress Information of the State of the Union, and recommend to their Consideration such Measures as he shall judge necessary and expedient; he may, on extraordinary Occasions, convene both Houses, or either of them, and in Case of Disagreement between them, with Respect to the Time of Adjournment, he may adjourn them to such Time as he shall think proper; he shall receive Ambassadors and other public Ministers; he shall take Care that the Laws be faithfully executed, and shall Commission all the Officers of the United States.

Section. 4.
The President, Vice President and all civil Officers of the United States, shall be removed from Office on Impeachment for, and Conviction of, Treason, Bribery, or other high Crimes and Misdemeanors.

ARTICLE. III.

Section. 1.
The judicial Power of the United States, shall be vested in one supreme Court, and in such inferior Courts as the Congress may from time to time ordain and establish. The Judges, both of the supreme and inferior Courts, shall hold their Offices during good Behaviour, and shall, at stated Times, receive for their Services, a Compensation, which shall not be diminished during their Continuance in Office.

Section. 2.
The judicial Power shall extend to all Cases, in Law and Equity, arising under this Constitution, the Laws of the United States, and Treaties made, or which shall be made, under their Authority;—to all Cases affecting Ambassadors, other public Ministers and Consuls;—to all Cases of admiralty and maritime Jurisdiction;—to Controversies to which the United States shall be a Party;—to Controversies between two or more States;— between a State and Citizens of another State,—between Citizens of different States,—between Citizens of the same State claiming Lands under Grants of different States, and between a State, or the Citizens thereof, and foreign States, Citizens or Subjects.

In all Cases affecting Ambassadors, other public Ministers and Consuls, and those in which a State shall be Party, the supreme Court shall have original Jurisdiction. In all the other Cases before mentioned, the supreme Court shall have appellate Jurisdiction, both as to Law and Fact, with such Exceptions, and under such Regulations as the Congress shall make.

The Trial of all Crimes, except in Cases of Impeachment, shall be by Jury; and such Trial shall be held in the State where the said Crimes shall have been committed; but when not committed within any State, the Trial shall be at such Place or Places as the Congress may by Law have directed.

Section. 3.

Treason against the United States, shall consist only in levying War against them, or in adhering to their Enemies, giving them Aid and Comfort. No Person shall be convicted of Treason unless on the Testimony of two Witnesses to the same overt Act, or on Confession in open Court.

The Congress shall have Power to declare the Punishment of Treason, but no Attainder of Treason shall work Corruption of Blood, or Forfeiture except during the Life of the Person attainted.

ARTICLE. IV.

Section. 1.

Full Faith and Credit shall be given in each State to the public Acts, Records, and judicial Proceedings of every other State. And the Congress may by general Laws prescribe the Manner in which such Acts, Records and Proceedings shall be proved, and the Effect thereof.

Section. 2.

The Citizens of each State shall be entitled to all Privileges and Immunities of Citizens in the several States.

A Person charged in any State with Treason, Felony, or other Crime, who shall flee from Justice, and be found in another State, shall on Demand of the executive Authority of the State from which he fled, be delivered up, to be removed to the State having Jurisdiction of the Crime.

No Person held to Service or Labour in one State, under the Laws thereof, escaping into another, shall, in Consequence of any Law or Regulation therein, be discharged from such Service or Labour, but shall be delivered up on Claim of the Party to whom such Service or Labour may be due.

Section. 3.

New States may be admitted by the Congress into this Union; but no new State shall be formed or erected within the Jurisdiction of any other State; nor any State be formed by the Junction of two or more States, or Parts of States, without the Consent of the Legislatures of the States concerned as well as of the Congress.

The Congress shall have Power to dispose of and make all needful Rules and

Regulations respecting the Territory or other Property belonging to the United States; and nothing in this Constitution shall be so construed as to Prejudice any Claims of the United States, or of any particular State.

Section. 4.

The United States shall guarantee to every State in this Union a Republican Form of Government, and shall protect each of them against Invasion; and on Application of the Legislature, or of the Executive (when the Legislature cannot be convened) against domestic Violence.

ARTICLE. V.

The Congress, whenever two thirds of both Houses shall deem it necessary, shall propose Amendments to this Constitution, or, on the Application of the Legislatures of two thirds of the several States, shall call a Convention for proposing Amendments, which, in either Case, shall be valid to all Intents and Purposes, as Part of this Constitution, when ratified by the Legislatures of three fourths of the several States, or by Conventions in three fourths thereof, as the one or the other Mode of Ratification may be proposed by the Congress; Provided that no Amendment which may be made prior to the Year One thousand eight hundred and eight shall in any Manner affect the first and fourth Clauses in the Ninth Section of the first Article; and that no State, without its Consent, shall be deprived of its equal Suffrage in the Senate.

ARTICLE. VI.

All Debts contracted and Engagements entered into, before the Adoption of this Constitution, shall be as valid against the United States under this Constitution, as under the Confederation.

This Constitution, and the Laws of the United States which shall be made in Pursuance thereof; and all Treaties made, or which shall be made, under the Authority of the United States, shall be the supreme Law of the Land; and the Judges in every State shall be bound thereby, any Thing in the Constitution or Laws of any State to the Contrary notwithstanding.

The Senators and Representatives before mentioned, and the Members of the several State Legislatures, and all executive and judicial Officers, both of the

United States and of the several States, shall be bound by Oath or Affirmation, to support this Constitution; but no religious Test shall ever be required as a Qualification to any Office or public Trust under the United States.

ARTICLE. VII.

The Ratification of the Conventions of nine States, shall be sufficient for the Establishment of this Constitution between the States so ratifying the Same.

The Word, "the," being interlined between the seventh and eighth Lines of the first Page, The Word "Thirty" being partly written on an Erazure in the fifteenth Line of the first Page, The Words "is tried" being interlined between the thirty second and thirty third Lines of the first Page and the Word "the" being interlined between the forty third and forty fourth Lines of the second Page.

Attest William Jackson Secretary done in Convention by the Unanimous Consent of the States present the Seventeenth Day of September in the Year of our Lord one thousand seven hundred and Eighty seven and of the Independance of the United States of America the Twelfth In witness whereof We have hereunto subscribed our Names,

G. Washington, Presidt and deputy from Virginia

Delaware
Geo: Read
Gunning Bedford jun
John Dickinson
Richard Bassett
Jaco: Broom

Maryland
James McHenry
Dan of St Thos. Jenifer
Danl. Carroll

Virginia
John Blair
James Madison Jr.

North Carolina
Wm. Blount
Richd. Dobbs Spaight
Hu Williamson

South Carolina
J. Rutledge
Charles Cotesworth Pinckney
Charles Pinckney
Pierce Butler

Georgia
William Few
Abr Baldwin

New Hampshire
John Langdon
Nicholas Gilman

Massachusetts
Nathaniel Gorham
Rufus King

Connecticut
Wm. Saml. Johnson
Roger Sherman

New York
Alexander Hamilton

New Jersey
Wil: Livingston
David Brearley
Wm. Paterson
Jona: Dayton

Pennsylvania
B Franklin
Thomas Mifflin
Robt. Morris
Geo. Clymer
Thos. FitzSimons
Jared Ingersoll
James Wilson
Gouv Morris

PRAYERLESSNESS

I shall need, too, the favor of that Being in whose hands we are . . . and to whose goodness I ask you to join with me in supplications.

—Thomas Jefferson

The worst sin is prayerlessness. Overt sin, or crime, or the glaring inconsistencies which often surprise us in Christian people are the effect of this, or its punishment. We are left by God for lack of seeking Him. The history of the saints shows often that their lapses were the fruit and nemesis of slackness or neglect in prayer. . . . Trusting the God of Christ, and transacting with Him, we come into tune with men. . . . Prayer is an act, indeed *the* act, of fellowship. We cannot truly pray even for ourselves without passing beyond ourselves and our individual experience. . . .

Not to want to pray, then, is the sin behind sin. And it ends in not being able to pray. . . . We do not take our spiritual food, and so we falter, dwindle, and die. "In the sweat of your brow ye shall eat your bread." That has been said to be true both of physical and spiritual labour.

—P. T. FORSYTH

PRAYER

Father, help me to persevere in my prayer life, so that I may grow closer to You. Amen.

URGED TO PRAY

The things that will destroy America are prosperity-at-any-price, peace-at-any-price, safety-first instead of duty-first, the love of soft living and the get-rich-quick theory of life.

—Theodore Roosevelt

The Lord told the story of a widow who wanted justice done to her enemy. By her unceasing requests, she persuaded an evil judge to listen to her. . . . The story encourages us that the Lord God, who is merciful and just, pays attention to our continual prayers more than when this widow won over the indifferent, unjust, and wicked judge by her unceasing requests. . . . The Lord gives a similar lesson in the parable of the man who had nothing to give to a traveling friend. . . . By his very urgent and insistent requests, he succeeded in waking the friend, who gave him as many loaves as he needed. But this friend was motivated by his wish to avoid further annoyances, not by generosity. Through this story the Lord taught that those who are asleep are compelled to give to the person who disturbs them, but those who never sleep will give with much more kindness. In fact, He even rouses us from sleep so that we can ask from Him.

—SAINT AUGUSTINE

PRAYER

Lord, thank You for urging me, continually reminding me of my need for Your presence. Amen.

HOPING AND PRAYING

We are all bound up together in one great bundle of humanity.

—Frances Ellen Watkins Harper

Let us realize that we can only fulfill our calling to bear much fruit, by praying much. In Christ are hid all the treasures men around us need; in Him all God's children are blessed with all spiritual blessings; He is full of grace and truth. But it needs prayer, much prayer, strong believing prayer, to bring these blessings down. . . .

Let us claim it as one of the revelations of our wonderful life in the Vine [Christ]: He tells us that if we ask in His name, in virtue of our union with Him, whatsoever it be, it will be done to us. Souls are perishing because there is too little prayer. God's children are feeble because there is too little prayer. We bear so little fruit because there is so little prayer. The faith of this promise [John 15:7] would make us strong to pray; let us not rest till it has entered into our very heart, and drawn us, in the power of Christ to continue and labor and strive in prayer until the blessing comes in power.

—ANDREW MURRAY

PRAYER

Heavenly Father, teach me to strive in prayer, to reach Your heart, and to draw from Your strength. Amen.

TURN YOUR GAZE UPON HIM

When you pray, rather let your heart be without words then your words without heart.

—John Bunyan

Jesus is passing through the crowd heading for the house of Jairus, so that He might raise the ruler's dead daughter. He is so extravagant in His goodness that He works another miracle on His way there. . . .

What delightful encouragement this truth affords us!

If our Lord is so ready to heal the sick and bless the needy, then, my soul, do not be slow to put yourself in His path so that He may smile on you. Do not be lazy in asking, since He is so generous in giving.

Pay careful attention to His Word now, and at all times, so that Jesus may speak through it to your heart. Pitch your tent wherever He is so that you can obtain His blessing. When He is present to heal, may He not heal you?

Be certain that He is present even now, for He always comes to hearts that need Him. And do you not need Him? He knows the extent of your need; so turn your gaze, look upon your distress, and call upon Him while He is near.

—ADAPTED FROM CHARLES SPURGEON

PRAYER

Lord, I call upon You while You are near. Thank You for hearing my prayer. Amen.

YOUR PRAYER HELPER

During the mid-1970s, as America wrestled with the aftermath of Watergate and sought national healing, President Gerald Ford turned to faith as a unifying force. In his National Day of Prayer Proclamation on December 5, 1974, Ford quoted President Dwight Eisenhower's 1955 declaration—words spoken during the Cold War: "Without God there could be no American form of government, nor an American way of life. Recognition of the Supreme Being is the first—the most basic—expression of Americanism. Thus, the founding fathers of America saw it, and thus with God's help, it will continue to be."

All true prayer is due to the influence of the Holy Spirit. The Holy Spirit not only guides you in the selection of the things for which to pray, but also gives you the appropriate desires. Please do not suppose that the Spirit itself prays or utters the inarticulate groans the apostle is speaking about here. The Spirit is said to do what the Spirit causes you to do. . . . More is meant here than that certain desires and feelings are awakened in your heart by a mere external influence. The Holy Spirit dwells inside the Christian believer as a principle of life.

—ADAPTED FROM CHARLES HODGE

PRAYER

Lord, I thank You for sending Your Spirit to intercede for me as I pray. Amen.

HOLD ON

Two works of mercy set a man free: forgive and you will be forgiven, and give and you will receive.

—Saint Augustine

The case of the Syrophoenician woman [Matthew 15:22] . . . is a notable instance of successful importunity, one which is eminently encouraging to all who would pray successfully. . . .

At first, Jesus appears to pay no attention to her agony, and ignores her cry for relief. He gives her neither eye, nor ear, nor word. Silence, deep and chilling, greets her impassioned cry. But she is not turned aside, nor disheartened. She holds on. . . .

This last cry won her case; her daughter was healed in the self-same hour. Hopeful, urgent, and unwearied, she stays near the master, insisting and praying until the answer is given. What a study in importunity, in earnestness, in persistence, promoted and propelled under conditions which would have disheartened any but a heroic, a constant soul.

—E. M. BOUNDS

PRAYER

Lord, teach me to hold on even when the answer to my prayer seems to be delayed. Amen.

A CITY UPON A HILL

For most of us the prayer in Gethsemane is the only model. Removing mountains can wait.

—C. S. Lewis

Ronald Reagan's "The Shining City Upon a Hill" speech, delivered on January 25, 1974, drew on an image first used by Puritan leader John Winthrop in 1630, who was quoting from a passage in the Bible (Matthew 5:14). Winthrop called the new Massachusetts Bay Colony "a city upon a hill," a symbol of American exceptionalism and a moral example to the world.

Reagan expanded on this, portraying America as a prosperous, free, and hopeful "shining city." His vision was inclusive, depicting a nation that welcomed people globally and stood as a beacon of freedom and opportunity for all.

We cannot escape our destiny, nor should we try to do so. The leadership of the free world was thrust upon us two centuries ago in that little hall of Philadelphia. In the days following World War II, when the economic strength and power of America was all that stood between the world and the return to the dark ages, Pope Pius XII said, "The American people have a great genius for splendid and unselfish actions. Into the hands of America God has placed the destinies of an afflicted mankind."

PRAYER

Lord, I pray that this great nation opens its hearts and minds to You and Your glory. Amen.

LISTENING FOR GOD

If the blind put their hand in God's, they find their way more surely than those who see but have no faith or purpose.

—Attributed to Helen Keller

There are times when solitude is better than society, and silence is wiser than speech. We should be better Christians if we were more alone, waiting upon God, and gathering, through meditation on His Word, spiritual strength for labor in His service. We ought to muse upon the things of God, because we thus get the real nutriment out of them.

. . . Our souls are not nourished merely by listening awhile to this, and then to that, and then to the other part of divine truth. Hearing, reading, marking, and learning, all require inwardly digesting to complete their usefulness, and the inward digesting of the truth lies for the most part in meditating upon it.

Why is it that some Christians, although they hear many sermons, make but slow advances in the divine life? Because they neglect their closets, and do not thoughtfully meditate on God's Word. They love the wheat, but they do not grind it; they would have the corn, but they will not go forth into the fields to gather it; the fruit hangs upon the tree, but they will not pluck it; the water flows at their feet, but they will not stoop to drink it. From such folly deliver us, O Lord.

—CHARLES SPURGEON

PRAYER

Lord, spare me from assigning Your name to the complex thoughts, desires, and motives of my own heart. Amen.

PRAY AND PREVAIL

The fundamental basis of this Nation's law was given to Moses on the Mount. The fundamental basis of our Bill of Rights comes from the teachings which we get from Exodus and St. Matthew, from Isaiah and St. Paul. . . . If we don't have the proper fundamental moral background, we will finally wind up with a totalitarian government which does not believe in rights for anybody except the state.

—Harry S. Truman

When Israel had made the golden calf, Moses returned to the Lord and said, "Oh, this people have sinned a great sin, and have made them gods of gold. Yet now, if thou wilt forgive their sin; and if not, blot me, I pray thee, out of thy book which thou hast written" (Exodus 32:31–32). That was persistence. Moses would rather have died than not have his people forgiven.

When God had heard him and said He would send His angel with the people, Moses came again. He would not be content until God Himself should go with them. God had said, "I will do this thing also that thou hast spoken" (Exodus 33:17). After that in answer to Moses' prayer, "I beseech thee, shew me thy glory" (Exodus 33:18), God made His goodness pass before him. Then Moses at once began pleading, "I pray thee, go among us" (Exodus 34:9). "And he was there with the Lord forty days and forty nights" (Exodus 34:28).

Moses was persistent with God and prevailed.

—ADAPTED FROM ANDREW MURRAY

PRAYER

Father, help me to have patience and to press on until the victory is won. Amen.

THREE PARTS

We have to pray with our eyes on God, not on the difficulties.

— **Oswald Chambers**

Christian freedom, in my opinion, consists of three parts. The first: that the consciences of believers, in seeking assurance of their justification before God, should rise above and advance beyond the law, forgetting all law righteousness. . . .

The second part, dependent upon the first, is that consciences observe the law, not as if constrained by the necessity of the law, but that freed from the law's yoke they willingly obey God's will. . . .

The third part of Christian freedom lies in this: regarding outward things that are of themselves "indifferent," we are not bound before God by any religious obligation preventing us from sometimes using them and other times not using them, indifferently. . . .

Accordingly, it is perversely interpreted both by those who allege it is an excuse for their desires that they may abuse God's good gifts to their own lust and by those who think that freedom does not exist unless it is used before men, and consequently, in using it have no regard for weaker brethren. . . . Nothing is plainer than this rule: that we should use our freedom if it results in the edification of our neighbor, but if it does not help our neighbor, then we should forego it.

—ADAPTED FROM JOHN CALVIN

PRAYER

Father, I pray that my heart never betrays You! I pray that this country never betrays You! Amen.

HEAVENLY HARMONY

With a good conscience our only sure reward, with history the final judge of our deeds, let us go forth to lead the land we love, asking His blessing and His help, but knowing that here on earth God's work must truly be our own.

—John F. Kennedy

Why did our Lord teach us to pray? In the same way the angels in heaven live in harmony, it is desirable for us to live together. Love is shared in heaven. There is agreement. Pride does not interfere. Nothing is pretended. These are things worth praying for here and now. . . .

"For as the body is one, and hath many members, and all the members of that one body, being many, are one body: so also is Christ" (1 Corinthians 12:12). You can do your part while others perform their function. The eye sees for the entire body. The hand works and the foot walks for the whole creature. If one member suffers, all suffer.

The ones who pray, therefore, should not criticize the ones who are busy working because they are not praying. The ones who toil are not to judge the ones who are at prayer because they are not working. Let everyone do whatever they are doing for the glory of God.

—ADAPTED FROM SAINT MACARIUS THE EGYPTIAN

PRAYER

Dear God, let me value the varied contributions of others. Amen.

OUR ALL

I used to ask God to help me. Then I asked if I might help Him. I ended up by asking Him to do His work through me.

—Attributed to Hudson Taylor

If Christ has our love, he has our all; and Christ never has what he deserves from us, till he has our love. True love withholds nothing from Christ, when it is sincerely set upon him. If we actually love him, he will have our time, and he will have our service, and he will have the use of all our resources, and gifts, and graces; indeed, then he shall have our possession, freedom, and our very lives, whenever he calls for them.

In the same way, when God loves any of us, he will withhold nothing from us that is good for us. He does not hold back his only begotten Son. When Christ loves us, he gives us everything we need—his merits to justify us, his Spirit to sanctify us, his grace to adorn us, and his glory to crown us. Therefore, when any of us love Christ sincerely, we lay everything down at his feet, and give up all to be at his command and service.

—ADAPTED FROM THOMAS DOOLITTLE

PRAYER

Lord, I know that when I come to You, You hear my prayers. I lay my burdens now at Your feet. Amen.

ALWAYS BE PRAYERFUL

The faith you mention has certainly its use in the world. . . . But I wish it were more productive of good works than I have generally seen it; I mean real good works; works of kindness, charity, mercy, and public spirit; not holiday keeping, sermon reading or hearing; performing church ceremonies, or making long prayers, filled with flatteries and compliments.

—**Benjamin Franklin**

Prayer is a preparation for danger, it is the armor for battle. Go not into the dangerous world without it. You kneel down at night to pray and drowsiness weighs down your eyelids. A hard day's work is a kind of excuse, and you shorten your prayer, and resign yourself softly to repose.

The morning breaks, and it may be you rise late, and so your early devotions are not done, or done with irregular haste. It is no marvel if that day in which you suffer drowsiness to interfere with prayer be a day on which you betray Him by cowardice and soft shrinking from duty.

—FREDERICK W. ROBERTSON

PRAYER

Lord, keep me from the temptation to shorten my prayer life, because that is where my strength comes from. Amen.

LITTLE EFFORT, BIG REWARD

Take a method and try it. If it fails, admit it frankly, and try another. But by all means, try something.

—Franklin D. Roosevelt

God does not lay a great burden on us—a little thinking of him, a little adoration, sometimes to pray for grace, sometimes to offer him your sorrows, sometimes to thank him for the good things he does.

Lift up your heart to him even at meals and when you are in company. The least little remembrance will always be acceptable to him. You don't have to be loud. He is nearer to us than you think.

You don't have to be in church all the time in order to be with God. We can make a chapel in our heart where we can withdraw from time to time and converse with him in meekness, humility, and love. Everyone has the capacity for such intimate conversation with God, some more, some less. He knows what we can do. Get started. Maybe he is just waiting for one strong resolution on your part. Have courage.

—ADAPTED FROM BROTHER LAWRENCE

PRAYER

Can it be that if I will make a little effort, my awareness of Your nearness will grow? Help me, Lord, to try. Amen.

STEADINESS IN PRAYER

In August 1862, President Abraham Lincoln confessed this: "I have been driven many times upon my knees by the overwhelming conviction that I had nowhere else to go. My own wisdom and that of all about me seemed insufficient for that day."

If we permit the love of God to replace our cares in this world, and if we give ourselves over to steady prayer and meditation, we will soon find our attitude and behavior changing. We will stop racing from one thing to another. We will rest in tranquility and peace.

A stable spiritual life requires much prayer and devout singing of psalms. Evil is only conquered by continual prayer.

Prayer can become habitual. Whether praying or meditating, it is possible to focus our attention on God. In this kind of prayer we do not think of anything in particular. Our whole will is directed toward God. The Holy Spirit burns in our soul. God is at the very heart of our being. Our prayers are made with affection and they become effective. If our prayers require words, we do not rush. We can offer almost every syllable as a prayer in itself. The love burning in us will give fiery life to our prayers.

Prayer of this kind is a delight.

—RICHARD ROLLE

PRAYER

Lord God, please fill my mind and give me a stability of spirit. Amen.

ABRAHAM LINCOLN'S GETTYSBURG ADDRESS

November 19, 1863

Four score and seven years ago our fathers brought forth, upon this continent, a new nation, conceived in Liberty, and dedicated to the proposition that all men are created equal.

Now we are engaged in a great civil war, testing whether that nation, or any nation so conceived, and so dedicated, can long endure. We are met here on a great battlefield of that war. We have come to dedicate a portion of it, as a final resting place for those who here gave their lives that that nation might live. It is altogether fitting and proper that we should do this.

But in a larger sense, we can not dedicate, we can not consecrate, we can not hallow this ground. The brave men, living and dead, who struggled here, have consecrated it far above our poor power to add or detract. The world will little note, nor long remember, what we say here, but can never forget what they did here.

It is for us, the living, rather to be dedicated here to the unfinished work which they have, thus far, so nobly carried on. It is rather for us to be here dedicated to the great task remaining before us that from these honored dead we take increased devotion to that cause for which they gave the last full measure of devotion that we here highly resolve that these dead shall not have died in vain; that this nation shall have a new birth of freedom; and that this government of the people, by the people, for the people, shall not perish from the earth.

PRAYER

Lord, I pray that You use me to make a difference in other people's lives. Amen.

PREPARING TO PRAY

No people can be bound to acknowledge and adore the Invisible Hand which conducts the affairs of men more than those of the United States.

—George Washington

God's Presence is universal. There is no place in the world—not one—that is devoid of God's Most Holy Presence. . . . This is a truth that all followers of Jesus readily admit, but all are not equally alive to its importance. . . . Because we are not seeing God with our physical eyes, we are too apt to forget God and act as though God is way far away.

While knowing perfectly well that God is everywhere, if we do not think about it, it is the same as if we did not know it. Therefore, before beginning to pray, it is always necessary to rouse your entire being to a constant, unswerving remembering and thinking about the Presence of God. In Old Testament days, when Jacob beheld the ladder that went up to heaven, he cried out, "Surely the Lord is in this place, and I wasn't even aware of it." By saying this, he meant that he had not thought about it, because, surely, he could not fail to know that God was everywhere and in all things. Therefore, when you are preparing to pray, you must say with your whole heart, "God is indeed here."

—ADAPTED FROM SAINT FRANCIS DE SALES

PRAYER

Father, as I prepare to enter Your presence, help me to say, "You are indeed here." I worship You in this place. Amen.

LOVE AND PRAYER

Friendship is the only cement that will ever hold the world together.

—**Woodrow Wilson**

Earnest prayer and fervent love are closely linked. If we pray only for ourselves, we will not find it easy to be in the right attitude toward God. But when our hearts are filled with love for others, we will continue to pray for them, even for those with whom we do not agree.

Prayer holds an important place in the life of love; they are inseparably connected. If you want your love to increase, forget yourself and pray for God's children. If you want to increase in prayerfulness, spend time loving those around you, helping to bear their burdens.

There is a great need for earnest, powerful intercessors! God desires His children to present themselves each day before the throne of grace to pray down the power of the Spirit upon all believers. . . .

As we meditate on love to those around us, we will be drawn into fellowship with God. . . . Love leads to prayer—to believing prayer is given the love of God.

—ANDREW MURRAY

PRAYER

Fill my heart with Your love for others, Lord. I want to be a burden-bearer, lifting others in prayer before You. Amen.

A LIFE OF PRAYER

You cannot divorce religious belief and public service. . . . I've never detected any conflict between God's will and my political duty. If you violate one, you violate the other.

—Jimmy Carter

Let us not be content to pray morning and evening, but let us live in prayer all day long. Let this prayer, this life of love, which means death to self, spread out from our seasons of prayer, as from a centre, over all that we have to do. All should become prayer, that is, a loving consciousness of God's presence, whether it be social intercourse or business. Such a course as this will ensure you a profound peace.

—FRANÇOIS FÉNELON

PRAYER

Lord, through my prayers I seek to be with You and to know Your peace all day long. Amen.

PRESSING INTO THE KINGDOM OF GOD

Do what you can, with what you've got, where you are.

—Quoted by Theodore Roosevelt

The kingdom of heaven should be sought, first, because of the extreme necessity we are in of getting into the kingdom of heaven. We are in a perishing necessity of it; without it we are utterly and eternally lost. . . . It should be sought, second, because of the shortness and uncertainty of the opportunity for getting into the kingdom. . . . There is much difficulty getting into the kingdom of God. Innumerable difficulties are in the way such as few conquer. Most of them who try do not have resolution, courage, earnestness, and constancy enough; but they fail, give up, and perish. . . .

Though it is attended with so much difficulty, yet it is not an impossible thing. God is able to accomplish it, and has sufficient mercy for it; and there is sufficient provision made through Christ that God may do it consistent with the honor of His majesty, justice, and truth. It is fitting that the kingdom should be thus sought because of the great excellency of it. We are willing to seek earthly things of trifling value; it therefore certainly becomes us to seek that with great earnestness which is of infinitely greater worth and excellence.

—ADAPTED FROM JONATHAN EDWARDS

PRAYER

Lord, I pray for Your will to be done in my life and in our nation today. Amen.

MAINTAIN INTEGRITY

If you learn it upon your knees you will never unlearn it.

—Charles Spurgeon

Hold fast your integrity, and rather let all go than let that go. A man had better let liberty, estate, relations, and life go, than let his integrity go. Yea, let ordinances themselves go, when they cannot be help with the hand of integrity: Job 27:5–6, "God forbid that I should justify you: till I die I will not remove mine integrity from me. My righteousness I hold fast, and will not let it go: my heart shall not reproach me so long as I live." Look, as the drowning man holds fast that which is cast forth for to save him, as the soldier hold fast his sword and buckler on which his life depends, so, saith Job, "I will hold fast my integrity; my heart shall not reproach me. I had rather all the world should reproach me; and my heart justify me, than that my heart should reproach me, and all the world justify me." That man will make but a sad exchange that shall exchange his integrity for any worldly concernment. Integrity maintained in the soul will be a feast of fat things in the worst of days; but let a man lose his integrity, and it is not in the power of all the world to make a feast of fat things in that soul.

—THOMAS BROOKS

PRAYER

Lord, help me to be a person of integrity! Help me to show You and only You to others. Amen.

LOVING OTHERS THROUGH PRAYER

Anything will give up its secrets if you love it enough. Not only have I found that when I talk to the little flower or to the little peanut it will give up its secrets, but I have found that when I silently commune with people they give up their secrets also—if you love them enough.

—George Washington Carver

As our great example in prayer, our Lord puts love as a primary condition—a love that has purified the heart from all the elements of hate, revenge, and ill will. Love is the supreme condition of prayer, a life inspired by love. . . .

Few, short, feeble prayers always betoken a low spiritual condition. Men ought to pray much and apply themselves to it with energy and perseverance. Eminent Christians have been eminent in prayer. The deep things of God are learned nowhere else. Great things for God are done by great prayers. He who prays much, studies much, loves much, works much, does much for God and humanity.

—E. M. BOUNDS

PRAYER

Lord, I want to be someone who does great things through prayer! Amen.

SOLITUDE AND SOCIETY

I would rather walk with God in the dark than go alone in the light.

—Mary Gardiner Brainard

If you are not under an obligation to mingle socially or entertain others in your home, remain within yourself. Entertain yourself. If visitors arrive or you are called out to someone for a good reason, go as one who is sent by God. Visit your neighbor with a loving heart and a good intention. . . .

In addition to a mental solitude to which you can retreat even in the middle of a crowd, learn to love actual physical solitude. There is no need to go out into the desert. Simply spend some quiet time alone in your room, in a garden, or some other place. There you can think some holy thoughts or do a little spiritual reading. One of the great bishops said, "I walk alone on the beach at sunset. I use such recreation to refresh myself and shake off a little of my ordinary troubles."

Our Lord received a glowing report from his apostles about how they had preached and what a great ministry they had done. Then he said to them, "Come ye yourselves apart into a desert place, and rest a while" (Mark 6:31).

—ADAPTED FROM SAINT FRANCIS DE SALES

PRAYER

Lord God, in good company or alone, let me be with You. Amen.

A PRAYER OF THANKS

I can only show my gratitude for these mercies from God, by a readiness to help His other children and my brethren. For I do not think that thanks and compliments, though repeated weekly, can discharge our real obligations to each other, and much less those to our Creator.

—Benjamin Franklin

Our Father, Thy children who know Thee delight themselves in Thy presence. We are never happier than when we are near Thee. We have found a little heaven in prayer. It has eased our load to tell Thee of its weight; it has relieved our wound to tell Thee of its smart. It has restored our spirit to confess to Thee its wanderings. No place like the Mercy Seat for us.

We thank Thee, Lord, that we have not only found benefit in prayer, but in the answers to it, we have been greatly enriched. Thou hast opened Thy hid treasures to the voice of prayer. Thou has supplied our necessities as soon as ever we have cried unto Thee. Yea, we have found it true, "Before they call I will answer, and while they are yet speaking I will hear" [Isaiah 65:24].

We do bless Thee, Lord, for instituting the blessed ordinance of prayer.

—CHARLES SPURGEON

PRAYER

Lord, thank You for the peace that transcends understanding when I pray to You. Amen.

OUR MORAL RESPONSIBILITIES

We must lay before him what is in us; not what ought to be in us.

—C. S. Lewis

President Harry S. Truman held office during the end of World War II. In this 1946 speech, he reminded Americans of what we fought for and how to preserve it:

We have just come through a decade in which forces of evil in various parts of the world have been lined up in a bitter fight to banish from the face of the earth . . . religion and democracy. For these forces of evil have long realized that both religion and democracy are rounded on one basic principle, the worth and dignity of the individual man and woman. Dictatorship, on the other hand, has always rejected that principle. Dictatorship, by whatever name, is rounded on the doctrine that the individual amounts to nothing; that the State is the only thing that counts; and that men and women and children were put on earth solely for the purpose of serving the State. . . .

If men and nations would but live by the precepts of the ancient prophets and the teachings of the Sermon on the Mount, problems which now seem so difficult would soon disappear. . . .

This is a supreme opportunity for the Church to continue to fulfill its mission on earth. . . . Oh, for an Isaiah or a Saint Paul to reawaken this sick world to its moral responsibilities!

PRAYER

Lord, I pray that this country embraces the teachings from Your Word and that our lives point toward You and You alone. Amen.

PRAY LIKE THIS

You can give without loving, but you cannot love without giving.

—Attributed to Amy Carmichael

No man will pray aright, unless his lips and heart shall be directed by the Heavenly Master. For that purpose he has laid down this rule, by which we must frame our prayers. . . .

This form of prayer consists, as I have said, of six petitions. The first three, it ought to be known, relate to the glory of God, without any regard to ourselves; and the remaining three relate to those things which are necessary for our salvation. As the law of God is divided into two tables, of which the former contains the duties of piety, and the latter the duties of charity, so in prayer Christ enjoins us to consider and seek the glory of God, and, at the same time, permits us to consult our own interests. Let us therefore know, that we shall be in a state of mind for praying in a right manner, if we not only are in earnest about ourselves and our own advantage, but assign the first place to the glory of God.

—JOHN CALVIN

PRAYER

Lord, teach me to pray as You would have me to pray. Amen.

FAITH AND HUMANITY

Prayer makes your heart bigger, until it is capable of containing the gift of God himself.

—Mother Teresa

With Hitler on the move in Europe, President Franklin D. Roosevelt said this in his 1939 State of the Union address:

Storms from abroad directly challenge three institutions indispensable to Americans, now as always. The first is religion. It is the source of the other two—democracy and international good faith.

Religion, by teaching man his relationship to God, gives the individual a sense of his own dignity and teaches him to respect himself by respecting his neighbors.

Democracy, the practice of self-government, is a covenant among free men to respect the rights and liberties of their fellows.

International good faith, a sister of democracy, springs from the will of civilized nations of men to respect the rights and liberties of other nations of men. . . .

There comes a time in the affairs of men when they must prepare to defend, not their homes alone, but the tenets of faith and humanity on which their churches, their governments and their very civilization are founded. The defense of religion, of democracy, and of good faith among nations is all the same fight. To save one we must now make up our minds to save all.

PRAYER

Lord, let me always consider You and others before myself. Amen.

IGNORANCE AND WEAKNESS

Only those who guide and those who follow, who take this providence of God from the source where it is authentic, have the happiness of knowing that there are those who seek life and know the lamp from which their spirits can be kindled is the lamp that glows in the Word of God.

—Woodrow Wilson

There are two causes of sin. Either we don't know what we ought to do or we refuse to do what we know we should. The first cause is ignorance. The second is weakness.

While we can fight against both, we will certainly be defeated unless God helps us. God can teach us what is right. As our knowledge of good and evil grows, God can help us to desire the better.

When we pray for forgiveness, we need to pray also that God will lead us away from sin. The psalmist sings, "The LORD is my light and my salvation" (Psalm 27:1). With light he takes away our ignorance. With salvation he strengthens us in weakness.

—ADAPTED FROM SAINT AUGUSTINE

PRAYER

O God, teach me Your law. Give me the strength to keep it. Amen.

PRAYING IN SECRET

So great is my veneration for the Bible . . . that the earlier my children begin to read it . . . the more lively and confident will be my hopes that they will prove useful citizens to their Country [and] respectful members of society.

—John Quincy Adams

When we pray, let our words and requests be disciplined, maintaining quietness and modesty. Let us consider ourselves as standing in God's sight. We must please the divine eyes both with the use of our body and with the tone of our voice. For, as it is characteristic for a shameless person to be noisy with his cries, it is fitting for the modest man to pray with calm requests. Moreover, the Lord told us to pray in secret, which is best suited to faith—in hidden and remote places and in our very bedrooms. Then we can know that God is present everywhere and hears and sees everything. In His abundant majesty, He enters even into hidden and secret places. It is written, "Am I a God at hand . . . and not a God afar off? Can any hide himself in secret places that I shall not see him? . . . Do not I fill heaven and earth?" (Jeremiah 23:23–24). And again: "The eyes of the Lord are in every place, beholding the evil and the good" (Proverbs 15:3).

—ADAPTED FROM SAINT CYPRIAN

PRAYER

Lord, I bring my requests quietly before You. In the stillness, I listen for Your voice. Amen.

THE DUTY OF PRAYER

My name is now Christian, but my name used to be Graceless.

—John Bunyan

The neglect of the duty of prayer seems to be inconsistent with supreme love to God also upon another account, and that is, that it is against the will of God so plainly revealed. —True love to God seeks to please him in every thing, and universally to conform to his will. . . .

Living in such a neglect is inconsistent with leading a holy life. . . .

A holy life is a life of faith. The life that true Christians live in the world, they live by the faith of the Son of God. But who can believe that the man lives by faith who lives without prayer, which is the natural expression of faith? Prayer is as natural an expression of faith, as breathing is of life; and to say a man lives a life of faith, and yet lives a prayerless life, is every whit as inconsistent and incredible, as to say, that a man lives without breathing. A prayerless life is so far from being a holy, that it is a profane life: he who lives so, lives like a heathen, who calleth not on God's name; he that lives a prayerless life, lives without God in the world.

—JONATHAN EDWARDS

PRAYER

Lord, help me to be always seeking You, living a life of faith and holiness. Amen.

FORGETTING TO PRAY

I am a firm believer in the Divine teachings, perfect example, and atoning sacrifice of Jesus Christ. I believe also in the Holy Scriptures as the revealed Word of God to the world for its enlightenment and salvation.

—Attributed to Rutherford B. Hayes

Lord, I confess this morning I remembered my breakfast but forgot my prayers. And as I have returned no praise, so thou mightest justly have afforded me no protection. Yet thou hast carefully kept me to the middle of the day, entrusted me with a new debt before I have paid the old score. It is now noon, too late for a morning, too soon for an evening, sacrifice. My corrupt heart prompts me to put off my prayers till night; but I know it too well, or rather too ill, to trust it. I fear, if till night I defer them, at night I shall forget them. Be pleased, therefore, now to accept them. Lord, let not a few hours the later make a breach; especially, seeing (being spoken not to excuse my negligence, but to implore thy pardon) a thousand years in thy sight are but as yesterday. I promise hereafter, by thy assistance, to bring forth fruit in due season.

—THOMAS FULLER

PRAYER

Lord, forgive my lapses of prayer, and help me to remember to put You first in my day. Amen.

RECOGNIZING GOD'S PRESENCE

I believe that God has planted in every heart the desire to live in freedom.

— George W. Bush

None but Jesus can give deliverance to captives. Real liberty cometh from Him only. It is a liberty righteously bestowed; for the Son, who is Heir of all things, has a right to make men free. The saints honor the justice of God, which now secures their salvation. It is a liberty which has been dearly purchased. Christ speaks it by His power, but He bought it by His blood. He makes thee free, but it is by His own bonds. Thou goest clear, because He bare thy burden for thee: thou art set at liberty, because He has suffered in thy stead. But, though dearly purchased, He freely gives it.

Jesus asks nothing of us as a preparation for this liberty. He finds us sitting in sackcloth and ashes, and bids us put on the beautiful array of freedom; He saves us just as we are, and all without our help or merit. When Jesus sets free, the liberty is perpetually entailed; no chains can bind again. . . . The world, with its temptations, may seek to ensnare us, but mightier is He who is for us than all they who be against us. . . . Our own deceitful hearts may harass and annoy us, but He who hath begun the good work in us will carry it on and perfect it to the end. The foes of God and the enemies of man may gather their hosts together, and come with concentrated fury against us, but if God acquitteth, who is he that condemneth?

—CHARLES SPURGEON

PRAYER

Lord, as I recognize Your presence in my daily life, draw me closer to You. I surrender myself to Your will. Amen.

GEORGE W. BUSH'S POST-9/11 SPEECH

September 11, 2001

On September 11, 2001, four American planes were hijacked and flown into buildings in the United States, killing nearly three thousand people. The world watched as four stories of the Pentagon fell onto the impact point, and the World Trade Center collapsed. That evening, President George W. Bush addressed the nation with a brief but powerful message, focusing on America's unity over fear:

These acts of mass murder were intended to frighten our nation into chaos and retreat. But they have failed; our country is strong.

A great people has been moved to defend a great nation. Terrorist attacks can shake the foundations of our biggest buildings, but they cannot touch the foundation of America. These acts shatter steel, but they cannot dent the steel of American resolve.

America was targeted for attack because we're the brightest beacon for freedom and opportunity in the world. And no one will keep that light from shining.

PRAYER

Lord, when all seems dark and evil around us, let this country come to You for guidance and strength. Amen.

THE TRUE PRAYER OF FAITH

My only hope of salvation is in the infinite, transcendent love of God manifested to the world by the death of His Son upon the cross. Nothing but His blood will wash away my sins. I rely exclusively upon it. Come, Lord Jesus! Come quickly!

—Benjamin Rush

One may ask if it wouldn't be better to make our wishes known to God, leaving it to Him to decide what is best, without seeking to assert our wills. The answer is: by no means. The prayer of faith which Jesus sought to teach His disciples does not simply proclaim its desire and then leave the decision to God. That would be the prayer of submission for cases in which we cannot know God's will. But the prayer of faith, finding God's will in some promise of the Word, pleads for that promise until it comes.

—ADAPTED FROM ANDREW MURRAY

PRAYER

Lord God, I pray for this country and thank You for the good work You began in it. Amen.

REALLY PRAYING THE LORD'S PRAYER

It is profitable for Christians to be often calling to mind the very beginnings of grace with their souls.

—John Bunyan

When I repeat the Lord's Prayer, my love causes me to desire to understand who this Father is and who this Master is who taught us the prayer.

You are wrong if you think you already know who he is. We should think of him every time we say his prayer. . . .

Imagine that Jesus taught this prayer to each one of us individually and that he continues to explain it to us. He is always close enough to hear us. To pray the Lord's Prayer well there is one thing you need to do. Stay near the side of the Master who taught it to you. . . .

Yes, it is a little troublesome to begin to consider Jesus when you pray the Lord's Prayer until it becomes habitual. You are right. This step turns vocal prayer into mental prayer. In my view, it is faithful vocal prayer. We need to think about who is listening to our prayers.

—ADAPTED FROM SAINT TERESA OF AVILA

PRAYER

Lord, I believe that You're leading me into deeper prayer. Help me really experience You. Amen.

WE LIVE

Man derives his greatest happiness not by that which he does for himself, but by what he accomplishes for others. . . . The most precious crown of fame that a human being can ask is to kneel at the bar of God and hear the beautiful words, "Well done, good and faithful servant."

—Schuyler Colfax

It is worthy of devout notice that Jesus touched the leper. This unclean person had broken through the regulations of the ceremonial law and pressed into the house, but Jesus so far from chiding him broke through the law himself in order to meet him.

He made an interchange with the leper, for while he cleansed him, he contracted by that touch a Levitical defilement. Even so Jesus Christ was made sin for us, although in himself he knew no sin, that we might be made the righteousness of God in him.

O that poor sinners would go to Jesus, believing in the power of his blessed substitutionary work, and they would soon learn the power of his gracious touch. That hand which multiplied the loaves, which saved sinking Peter, which upholds afflicted saints, which crowns believers, that same hand will touch every seeking sinner, and in a moment make him clean.

The love of Jesus is the source of salvation. He loves, he looks, he touches us, we live.

—CHARLES SPURGEON

PRAYER

Jesus, You, who knew no sin, became sin for me. You are my salvation, Lord, and my very life. Amen.

ABIDETH FOREVER

A habit of prayer is one of the surest marks of a true Christian.

—J. C. Ryle

Let us consider one another. He that enters into the Holiest enters into the home of eternal love; the air he breathes there is love; the highest blessing he can receive there is a heart in which the love of God is shed abroad in power by the Holy Ghost, and which is on the path to be made perfect in love. *That you may know how you ought to behave thyself in the house of God*—remember this: *Faith and hope shall pass away but love abides ever. The chief of these is love.*

Let us consider one another. When first we seek the entrance into the Holiest, the thought is merely of ourselves. And when we have entered in in faith, it is as if it is all we can do to stand before God, and wait on Him for what He has promised to do for us. But it is not long before we perceive that the Holiest and the Lamb are not for us alone; that there are others within with whom it is blessed to have fellowship in praising God; that there are some without who need our help to be brought in.

—ANDREW MURRAY

PRAYER

Lord, may I forever be at Your feet, clinging to Your righteousness! Amen.

LOVE AND PRAYERS

I now make it my earnest prayer, that God would have you, and the State over which you preside, in his holy protection; that he would incline the hearts of the Citizens to cultivate a spirit of subordination and obedience to Government, to entertain a brotherly affection and love for one another, for their fellow Citizens of the United States at large, and particularly for brethren who have served in the Field.

—George Washington

We are all selfish by nature, and our selfishness is very apt to stick to us, even when we are converted. There is a tendency in us to think only of our own souls, our own spiritual conflicts, our own progress in religion, and to forget others. Against this tendency we all have need to watch and strive, and not the least in our prayers. . . . We should try to bear in our hearts the whole world, the [unbelievers], . . . the body of true believers, the [churches], the country in which we live, the household in which we sojourn, the friends and relatives we are connected with. For each and all of these we should plead. This is the highest charity. They love me best who loves me in their prayers.

—J. C. RYLE

PRAYER

Lord, take away selfishness from my life and from our nation. Help us to focus on the needs of others. Amen.

CHRISTIAN MEDITATION

If we and our posterity neglect [the Bible's] instructions and authority, no man can tell how sudden a catastrophe may overwhelm us and bury all our glory in profound obscurity.

—Daniel Webster

Read a passage from the Gospels. Imagine the scene as though it were actually taking place in front of you. Place yourself, for instance, at the foot of the cross. This will prevent your mind from wandering the same way a cage restricts a bird.

After your imagination has helped you prepare yourself, begin to meditate mentally. If a particular thought catches your interest, stay with it. The bees do not flit from flower to flower. They stay until they have gathered all the honey they can from each. If you find nothing after trying a particular thought, move on to the next. But don't rush the process. . . .

Conclude your meditations with humble thanks and an offering of yourself to God. Offer prayers and then gather a devotional nosegay. Let me explain what I mean by that. When people have been strolling through a beautiful garden, they usually pick four or five flowers to take with them through the day. . . . When our souls have roamed in meditation through a spiritual garden, we can choose two or three ideas that seemed most helpful and think about them occasionally all day long.

—ADAPTED FROM SAINT FRANCIS DE SALES

PRAYER

Lord God,
I know that
simplicity
is possible.
Please give
me a single-
minded focus
on You. Amen.

DIVINE HAND

I would rather be what God chose to make me than the most glorious creature that I could think of; for to have been born in God's thought, and then made by God is the dearest, grandest, and most precious thing in all thinking. This is a prayer of contentment.

—C. S. Lewis

On March 5, 1877, Rutherford B. Hayes stated the following during his Inaugural Address:

Looking for the guidance of that Divine Hand by which the destinies of nations and individuals are shaped, I call upon you, Senators, Representatives, judges, fellow citizens, here and everywhere, to unite with me in an earnest effort to secure to our country the blessings, not only of material property, but of justice, peace, and union—a union depending not upon the constraint of force, but upon the loving devotion of a free people; "and that all things may be so ordered and settled upon the best and surest foundations that peace and happiness, truth and justice, religion and piety, may be established among us for all generations."

PRAYER

Lord, I give You full devotion and praise for all that You are! Amen.

THE PRAYER THAT DRAWS OTHERS TO GOD

Thy prayers are all filed in heaven, and if not immediately answered , they are certainly not forgotten, but in a little while shall be fulfilled to thy delight and satisfaction.

—Charles Spurgeon

One way is clear: the prayer will react upon the mind that prays, its light will grow, will shine the brighter, and draw and enlighten the more. But there must be more in the thing. Prayer in its perfect idea of being a rising up into the will of the Eternal, may not the help of the Father become one with the prayer of the child, and for the prayer of him he holds in his arms, go forth from him who wills not yet to be lifted to his embrace? To his bosom God himself cannot bring his children at once, and not at all except through his own suffering and theirs. But will not any good parent find some way of granting the prayer of the child who comes to him, saying, "Papa, this is my brother's birthday: I have nothing to give him, and I do love him so! could you give me something to give him, or give him something for me?"

—GEORGE MACDONALD

PRAYER

Father God, today I lift those I love in prayer. I pray they would know You more deeply. Amen.

PASSIONATE PRAYERS

Few will have the greatness to bend history; but each of us can work to change a small portion of the events, and in the total of all these acts will be written the history of this generation. . . . It is from numberless diverse acts of courage such as these that the belief that human history is thus shaped.

—Robert F. Kennedy

Ardent desire is the basis of unceasing prayer. It is not a shallow, fickle inclination, but a strong yearning, an unquenchable ardor, which impregnates, glows, burns, and fixes the heart. It is the flame of a present and active principle mounting up to God. It is ardor propelled by desire, that burns its way to the throne of mercy, and gains its plea. It is the pertinacity of desire that gives triumph to the conflict, in a great struggle of prayer. It is the burden of a weighty desire that sobers, makes restless, and reduces to quietness the soul just emerged from its mighty wrestlings. It is the embracing character of desire which arms prayer with a thousand pleas, and robes it with an invincible courage and an all-conquering power.

—E. M. BOUNDS

PRAYER

Lord God, I pray that You would rekindle a new love for You in the hearts of Americans. Remind us of the goodness of knowing You. Amen.

A CHANCE TO BLESS

No people ought to feel greater obligations to celebrate the goodness of the Great Disposer of events, and of the destiny of nations, than the people of the United States. . . . And to the same Divine Author of every good and perfect gift, we are indebted for all those privileges and advantages, religious as well as civil, which are so richly enjoyed in this favored land.

—James Madison

Are you encompassed with needs at this very moment, and almost overwhelmed with difficulties, trials, and emergencies? These are all divinely provided vessels for the Holy Spirit to fill, and if you but rightly understood their meaning, they would become opportunities for receiving new blessings and deliverances which you can get in no other way.

Bring these vessels to God. Hold them steadily before Him in faith and prayer. Keep still, and stop your own restless working until He begins to work. Do nothing that He does not Himself command you to do. Give Him a chance to work, and He will surely do so; and the very trials that threatened to overcome you with discouragement and disaster, will become God's opportunity for the revelation of His grace and glory in your life, as you have never known Him before.

—A. B. SIMPSON

PRAYER

Lord, I bring the needs of this country to You. Please work in our lives to bring You glory and honor. Amen.

LOVE CONQUERS SELFISHNESS

T'wan't me, 'twas de Lord! I always tole him, "I trust to you. I don't know where to go or what to do, but I expect you to lead me," an' he always did.

—Harriet Tubman

N*othing but love can expel and conquer our selfishness.* Self is the great curse, whether in its relation to God or to our fellow-men in general, or to fellow-Christians, thinking of ourselves and seeking our own. Self is our greatest curse. But, praise God, Christ came to redeem us from self. . . . Deliverance from self-life means to be a vessel overflowing with love to everybody all the day.

Many people pray for the power of the Holy Spirit, and they get something, but oh, so little! because they prayed for power for work, and power for blessing, but they have not prayed for power for full deliverance from self. . . .

A great many of us try hard at times to love. We try to force ourselves to love, and I do not say that is wrong; it is better than nothing. But the end of it is always very sad. "I fail continually," such a one must confess. . . .

And how can I learn to love? Never until the Spirit of God fills my heart with God's love, and I begin to long for God's love in a very different sense from which I have sought it so selfishly, as a comfort and a joy and a happiness and a pleasure to myself.

—ANDREW MURRAY

PRAYER

Heavenly Father, fill my heart with Your love so that nothing of my own selfishness remains. Amen.

LOOK UPON THEM

When we speak with God, our power of addressing Him, of holding communion with Him, and listening to His still small voice, depends upon our will being one and the same with His.

—Florence Nightingale

Look upon all the things of this world as you will look upon them when you come to die. At what a poor rate do men look on the things of this world when they come to die! What a low value do men set upon the pomp and glory of it, when there is but a step between them and eternity! Men may now put a mask upon them, but then they will appear in their own colours. Men would not venture the loss of such great things for them did they but look on them now, as they will do at the last day.

—THOMAS BROOKS

PRAYER

Lord, may I die with my hands open to all those around me. May I never put things above You. Amen.

NEEDS SUPPLIED

Can the liberties of a nation be secure when we have removed a conviction that these liberties are the gift of God?

—**Thomas Jefferson**

If it be a throne of grace, then *all the wants of those who come to it will be supplied*. The King from off such a throne will not say, "Thou must bring to Me gifts; thou must offer to Me sacrifices." It is not a throne for receiving tribute; it is a throne for dispensing gifts. Come then, ye who are poor as poverty itself; come ye that have no merits and are destitute of virtues; come ye that are reduced to a beggarly bankruptcy by Adam's fall and by your own transgressions. . . . Come ye, now, and receive the wine and milk which are freely given, yea, come, buy wine and milk without money and without price. All the petitioner's wants shall be supplied, because it is a throne of grace.

—CHARLES SPURGEON

PRAYER

Lord, I approach Your throne with confidence, knowing that You receive me in Your love. Amen.

THE SPIRIT OF PRAYER

In times of affliction we commonly meet with the sweetest experiences of the love of God.

—John Quincy Adams

The spirit of prayer is a holy spirit, a gracious spirit. . . . Wherever there is a true spirit of supplication, there is the spirit of grace. The true spirit of prayer is no other than God's own spirit dwelling in the hearts of the saints. And as this spirit comes from God, so doth it naturally tend to God in holy breathings and pantings. It naturally leads to God to converse with him by prayer. Therefore the Spirit is said to make intercession for the saints with groanings which cannot be uttered, Romans 8:26.

The Spirit of God makes intercession for them, as it is that Spirit which in some respect [incites] their prayers, and leads them to pour out their souls before God. Therefore the saints are said to worship God in the spirit; Philippians 3:3: "We are the circumcision, who worship God in the Spirit;" and John 4:23: "The true worshippers worship the Father in spirit and in truth." The truly godly have the spirit of adoption, the spirit of a child, to which it is natural to go to God and call upon him, crying to him as to a father.

—JONATHAN EDWARDS

PRAYER

Lord, I pray for a true spirit of prayer to be evident in my life. Amen.

THE TRANSFORMATIONAL JOURNEY OF THE BILL OF RIGHTS

After the Revolutionary War, the United States faced a tough task. They needed a government to unite the states while also protecting people's freedoms. This struggle led to the creation of the Bill of Rights.

James Madison, the father of the United States Constitution, considered people's desires and fears. In response, he wrote the first ten amendments to protect Americans' rights: freedom of speech, religion, and the press; the right to assemble and speak up; safeguards against unfair searches; fair trials; limits on harsh punishment; and reserved rights for states and individuals.

These rights were more than just words on paper. They protected everyday people. Families could practice their religion freely. Newspaper reporters could question those in power. People could come together to ask for change without being afraid. Soldiers could not just walk into homes. Anyone accused of a crime had the right to defend themselves in court.

The Bill of Rights was adopted on December 15, 1791. It significantly changed the Constitution, making the government a true protector of freedom.

PRAYER

Lord, let us not take for granted the rights we've been given in our nation, and help us use those rights to serve You. Amen.

THE BILL OF RIGHTS

Congress of the United States begun and held at the City of New-York, on Wednesday the fourth of March, one thousand seven hundred and eighty nine.

THE Conventions of a number of the States, having at the time of their adopting the Constitution, expressed a desire, in order to prevent misconstruction or abuse of its powers, that further declaratory and restrictive clauses should be added: And as extending the ground of public confidence in the Government, will best ensure the beneficent ends of its institution.

RESOLVED by the Senate and House of Representatives of the United States of America, in Congress assembled, two thirds of both Houses concurring, that the following Articles be proposed to the Legislatures of the several States, as amendments to the Constitution of the United States, all, or any of which Articles, when ratified by three fourths of the said Legislatures, to be valid to all intents and purposes, as part of the said Constitution; viz.

ARTICLES in addition to, and Amendment of the Constitution of the United States of America, proposed by Congress, and ratified by the Legislatures of the several States, pursuant to the fifth Article of the original Constitution.

Article the first . . . After the first enumeration required by the first article of the Constitution, there shall be one Representative for every thirty thousand, until the number shall amount to one hundred, after which the proportion shall be so regulated by Congress, that there shall be not less than one hundred Representatives, nor less than one Representative for every forty thousand persons, until the number of Representatives shall amount to two hundred; after which the proportion shall be so regulated by Congress, that there shall not be less than two hundred Representatives, nor more than one Representative for every fifty thousand persons.

Article the second . . . No law, varying the compensation for the services of the Senators and Representatives, shall take effect, until an election of Representatives shall have intervened.

Article the third . . . Congress shall make no law respecting an establishment of religion, or prohibiting the free exercise thereof; or abridging the freedom of speech, or of the press; or the right of the people peaceably to assemble, and to petition the Government for a redress of grievances.

Article the fourth . . . A well regulated Militia, being necessary to the security of a free State, the right of the people to keep and bear Arms, shall not be infringed.

Article the fifth . . . No Soldier shall, in time of peace be quartered in any house, without the consent of the Owner, nor in time of war, but in a manner to be prescribed by law.

Article the sixth . . . The right of the people to be secure in their persons, houses, papers, and effects, against unreasonable searches and seizures, shall not be violated, and no Warrants shall issue, but upon probable cause, supported by Oath or affirmation, and particularly describing the place to be searched, and the persons or things to be seized.

Article the seventh . . . No person shall be held to answer for a capital, or otherwise infamous crime, unless on a presentment or indictment of a Grand Jury, except in cases arising in the land or naval forces, or in the Militia, when in actual service in time of War or public danger; nor shall any person be subject for the same offence to be twice put in jeopardy of life or limb; nor shall be compelled in any criminal case to be a witness against himself, nor be deprived of life, liberty, or property, without due process of law; nor shall private property be taken for public use, without just compensation.

Article the eighth . . . In all criminal prosecutions, the accused shall enjoy the right to a speedy and public trial, by an impartial jury of the State and district wherein the crime shall have been committed, which district shall have been previously ascertained by law, and to be informed of the nature and cause of the accusation; to be confronted with the witnesses against him; to have compulsory process for obtaining witnesses in his favor, and to have the Assistance of Counsel for his defence.

Article the ninth . . . In suits at common law, where the value in controversy shall exceed twenty dollars, the right of trial by jury shall be preserved, and no fact tried by a jury, shall be otherwise re-examined in any Court of the United States, than according to the rules of the common law.

Article the tenth . . . Excessive bail shall not be required, nor excessive fines imposed, nor cruel and unusual punishments inflicted.

Article the eleventh . . . The enumeration in the Constitution, of certain rights, shall not be construed to deny or disparage others retained by the people.

Article the twelfth . . . The powers not delegated to the United States by the Constitution, nor prohibited by it to the States, are reserved to the States respectively, or to the people.

ATTEST,

Frederick Augustus Muhlenberg, Speaker of the House of Representatives

John Adams, Vice-President of the United States, and President of the Senate

John Beckley, Clerk of the House of Representatives.

Sam. A Otis Secretary of the Senate

OFFERING OURSELVES

Freedom is indivisible, and when one man is enslaved, all are not free.

—John F. Kennedy

Has [God] written thy name in His book of life? Has He given thee countless blessings? Has He laid up for thee a store of mercies, which eye hath not seen nor ear heard? Then do something for Jesus worthy of His love. Give not a mere wordy offering to a dying Redeemer.

How will you feel when your Master comes, if you have to confess that you did nothing for Him, but kept your love shut up, like a stagnant pool, neither flowing forth to His poor or to His work. Out on such love as that! What do men think of a love which never shows itself in action? Why, they say, "Open rebuke is better than secret love." Who will accept a love so weak that it does not actuate you to a single deed of self-denial, of generosity, of heroism, or zeal? Think how He has loved you, and given Himself for you! Do you know the power of that love? Then let it be like a rushing mighty wind to your soul, to sweep out the clouds of your worldliness, and clear away the mists of sin.

—CHARLES SPURGEON

PRAYER

Jesus, it is truly nothing to lose luxury, fame, money, or life if I have You. Enable this country to lose itself in You. Amen.

WHY PRAY?

Hold fast to the Bible as the sheet-anchor of your liberties; write its precepts in your hearts, and practice them in your lives.

—Ulysses S. Grant

Although it is true that while we are listless or insensible to our wretchedness, he wakes and watches for us and sometimes even assists us unasked; it is very much for our interest to be constantly supplicating him; first, that our heart may always be inflamed with a serious and ardent desire of seeking, loving and serving him, while we accustom ourselves to have recourse to him as a sacred anchor in every necessity; secondly, that no desires, no longing whatever, of which we are ashamed to make him the witness, may enter our minds, while we learn to place all our wishes in his sight, and thus pour out our heart before him; and, lastly, that we may be prepared to receive all his benefits with true gratitude and thanksgiving, while our prayers remind us that they proceed from his hand.

Moreover, having obtained what we asked, being persuaded that he has answered our prayers, we are led to long more earnestly for his favour, and at the same time have greater pleasure in welcoming the blessings which we perceive to have been obtained by our prayers.

—JOHN CALVIN

PRAYER

Lord, I lay all my desires before You and submit myself to You. Amen.

TO BE WISE

None can believe how powerful prayer is, and what it is able to effect, but those who have learned it by experience.

—Martin Luther

There cannot anything be imagined more absurd in itself, than wise, and sublime, and heavenly prayers, added to a life of vanity and folly, where neither labour nor diversions, neither time nor money, are under the direction of the wisdom and heavenly tempers of our prayers. If we were to see a man pretending to act wholly with regard to God in everything that he did, that would neither spend time nor money, not take any labour or diversion, but so far as he could act according to strict principles of reason and piety, and yet at the same time neglect all prayer, whether public or private, should we not be amazed at such a man, and wonder how he could have so much folly along with so much religion?

—WILLIAM LAW

PRAYER

Lord, I pray for wisdom for this country, and that Americans will walk away from the folly surrounding us. Amen.

TINY PRAYERS

I love to think of nature as unlimited broadcasting stations, through which God speaks to us every day, every hour and every moment of our lives, if we will only tune in and remain so.

—George Washington Carver

Make frequent, short little prayers to God. Express your appreciation for his beauty. Ask him to help you. Fall at the foot of the cross. Love his goodness. Give your soul to him a thousand times a day. Stretch out your hand to him like a child. If such prayerful, intimate thoughts become habitual, you will gain a beautiful familiarity with God. . . .

On one very clear night a devout person stood by a brook watching the sky. The stars were reflected in the water. That person said, "O my God, in the same way the stars of heaven are reflected here on earth, so are we on earth reflected in heaven." Saint Francis knelt in prayer beside such a beautiful brook and became enraptured. "God's grace flows as gently and sweetly as this little stream." Another saint watched a mother hen gather little chickens under her. He said, "Lord, keep us all under the shadow of your wings." . . .

Many little prayers like this can make up for the lack of all other prayers. They are essential. Without them rest is mere idleness and labor is pure drudgery.

—ADAPTED FROM SAINT FRANCIS DE SALES

PRAYER

Lord, I give You my day and ask You to reveal Yourself to me in the smallest of things. Amen.

HE IS OUR EXAMPLE

I am not only willing to fight for liberty, but to prove that courage knows no gender.

—Attributed to Deborah Sampson

Prayer alone prevails over God. But Christ has willed that it doesn't operate for evil. He gave it all its virtue when used for good. And so it knows only . . . how to transform the weak, restore the sick, purge the possessed, open prison bars, and loosen the bonds of the innocent. Likewise, it washes away faults, repels temptations, extinguishes persecutions, consoles the faint-spirited, cheers the down-trodden, escorts travelers, calms waves, frightens robbers, nourishes the poor, governs the rich, raises the fallen, rescues the falling, confirms the standing. Prayer is the wall of faith. It arms us and hurls missiles against the enemy who watches us on all sides. So we never walk unarmed. By day, we are aware of our post—by night, of our vigil. Under the armor of prayer, we guard the banner of our General. We wait in prayer for the angel's trumpet. . . . What more do we need then, but the duty of prayer? Even the Lord Himself prayed, to whom be honor and virtue for ages and ages!

—ADAPTED FROM TERTULLIAN

PRAYER

Father, amazing things happen when we pray. Help this great nation give thanks to You each day. Amen.

GOD'S WORK IN US

God sells us all good things at the price of labor.

—Leonardo da Vinci

Prayer is not our work, but God's work, which He works within us by His almighty power. As we consider this statement, our attitude should be one of silent expectation that as we pray, the Holy Spirit will help in our weakness and pray within us with "groanings that cannot be uttered" [Romans 8:26].

What a thought! When I feel how defective my prayers are, when I have no strength of my own, I may bow in silence before God in the confidence that His Holy Spirit will teach me to pray. The Spirit is the Spirit of prayer. It is not my work, but God's work in me. My desire to pray is a sign that God will hear me. . . .

The Spirit will perfect the work, even in our weakness. . . .

I have already told you about the Spirit of truth, who will glorify Christ in us, and of the Spirit of love, who will pour out this love in our hearts. Now we have the Spirit of prayer, through whom our lives may be ones of continual prayer. Thank God. The Spirit has been given from heaven to dwell in our hearts and to teach us to pray.

—ANDREW MURRAY

PRAYER

Work through me, O Lord. Pray through me, Holy Spirit. I am Your willing vessel. Amen.

AN UNALIENABLE RIGHT

When I pray for another person, I am praying for God to open my eyes so that I can see that person as God does, and then enter into the stream of love that God already directs toward that person.

— **Philip Yancey**

In James Madison's 1785 petition, *Memorial and Remonstrance Against Religious Assessments*, he wrote the following:

The Religion then of every man must be left to the conviction and conscience of every man; and it is the right of every man to exercise it as these may dictate. This right is in its nature an unalienable right. It is unalienable, because the opinions of men, depending only on the evidence contemplated by their own minds cannot follow the dictates of other men: It is unalienable also, because what is here a right towards men, is a duty towards the Creator. It is the duty of every man to render to the Creator such homage and such only as he believes to be acceptable to him. This duty is precedent, both in order of time and in degree of obligation, to the claims of Civil Society. Before any man can be considered as a member of Civil Society, he must be considered as a subject of the Governour of the Universe.

PRAYER

Lord, I lay my heart at Your feet and pray that You will lead me only on a path toward You. Amen.

PRAYING NATURALLY

Love divine, all loves excelling, Joy of Heav'n to Earth come down. Fix in us thy humble dwelling, All thy faithful mercies crown.

—Charles Wesley

Prayer is a longing, a desire of the spirit toward God. It is like someone who is sick longing for health.

Faith prays constantly. The spirit is always attentive to the will of God and knows its own fragility. It also remembers the infirmities of others, understanding that there is no strength and no help anywhere other than in God. A neighbor's grief is no less than your own.

Suppose someone who is weak in the faith asks for your prayers. Lead such a person to the truth and promises of God. Teach that person how to trust God.

If you give me a thousand dollars and ask me to pray for you, I am no more bound than I was before. I could not pray more for you if you gave me all the world. If I see a need, I pray. I can't help praying when God's Spirit is in me.

—ADAPTED FROM WILLIAM TYNDALE

PRAYER

Dear God, let prayer become a natural thing for me. Let my prayers flow like a river between us. Amen.

THE MOST PERFECT PRAYERS

All must admit that the reception of the teachings of Christianity results in the purest patriotism, in the most scrupulous fidelity to public trust, and in the best type of citizenship.

—Grover Cleveland

God's command to "pray without ceasing" is founded on the necessity we have of His grace to preserve the life of God in the soul, which can no more subsist one moment without it, than the body can without air. Whether we think of or speak to God, whether we act or suffer for Him, all is prayer, when we have no other object than His love, and the desire of pleasing Him. . . .

Prayer continues in the desire of the heart though the understanding be employed on outward things.

In souls filled with love, the desire to please God is a continual prayer. . . . God only requires of His adult children that their hearts be truly purified, and that they offer Him continually the wishes and vows that naturally spring from perfect love. For these desires, being the genuine fruits of love, are the most perfect prayers that can spring from it.

—JOHN WESLEY

PRAYER

God, please guide this country as we seek to think about Your great mercies throughout the day. Amen.

OUR WHOLE HEART

We all agree in the obligation of the moral precepts of Jesus, and nowhere will they be found delivered in greater purity than in his discourses.

—Thomas Jefferson

Your will be done, on earth as it is in heaven.

May we love you with our whole heart by always thinking of you, with our whole soul by always desiring you, with our whole mind by directing all our intentions to you, and with our whole strength by spending all our energies in your service. And may we love our neighbors as ourselves. . . .

Give us this day our daily bread.

In memory and understanding and reverence of the love which our Lord Jesus Christ has for us, revealed by his sacrifice for us on the cross, we ask for the perfect bread of his body.

And forgive us our trespasses.

We know that you forgive us, through the suffering and death of your beloved Son.

As we forgive those who trespass against us.

Enable us to forgive perfectly and without reserve any wrong that has been committed against us.

—ADAPTED FROM SAINT FRANCIS OF ASSISI

PRAYER

Lord, help this country pray this prayer, searching for You daily. Amen.

CAN PRAYER BE PUT INTO WORDS?

It is my duty, said he, to distrust mine own ability, that I may have reliance on him that is stronger than all.

—John Bunyan

It is best for a soul not to attempt to rise by its own efforts. If the well is dry, we are not able to put water into it. Pay attention to this. If the soul tries to go forward, it may actually go backward. The foundation for prayer is humility. The nearer we come to God, the more humility we need. There is a kind of pride that makes us want to be more spiritual. God is already doing more for us than we deserve.

When I say that people should not attempt to rise unless they are raised by God, I am using spiritual language. Some will understand me. If you can't understand what I am saying, I don't know another way to explain it.

I am sorry for those who begin with only books. There is a big difference between understanding something and knowing it through experience. I have read many religious books that deal with these matters. They explain very little. If one's soul has not already accumulated some practice in prayer, books are not much help.

—ADAPTED FROM SAINT TERESA OF AVILA

PRAYER

Lord, I know You hear the words of my prayers and all the prayers of our nation. Be with us now as we pray. Amen.

CHRIST-CONSCIOUSNESS

Brief prayers . . . pregnant with the Spirit, strongly fortified by faith . . . the fewer the words, the better the prayer. The more the words, the worse the prayer. Few words and much meaning is Christian. Many words and little meaning is pagan.

—Martin Luther

If one is really united to Christ in a union so established that Christ is indeed in possession of the soul, the whole consciousness will be taken up with what I would call Christ-consciousness, and there will be no self-consciousness. Little children are very prompt to show their character. There is a great difference in them. Bring a child into a room. She comes thinking about nothing in particular, looking at her mother, then looking at the guests or anything that objectively strikes her, not thinking of herself. That is pure, sweet, and lovely. She grows older, and she comes to think of herself and what people think of her, and her manner has lost its unconsciousness. A great deal of what you call bashfulness is rottenness at the heart; it is self-consciousness. Nothing in the world so tends to defile the imagination, to pervert the affections, and to corrupt the morals, as self-consciousness. You know it is connected with every diseased and morbid action of the body.

—A. A. HODGE

PRAYER

Connect me, O Lord, to Your heart and Your desires. May I walk with You until my last day on earth. Amen.

NEARER, NEARER

At any price, give me the book of God! I have it: Here is knowledge enough for me. Let me be homo unius libri: "A man of one book."

—John Wesley

"Grow in grace" [2 Peter 3:18]—not in one grace only, but in all grace. Grow in that root-grace, *faith*. Believe the promises more firmly than you have done. Let faith increase in fulness, constancy, simplicity.

Grow also in *love*. Ask that your love may become extended, more intense, more practical, influencing every thought, word, and deed.

Grow likewise in humility. Seek to lie very low, and know more of your own nothingness. As you grow downward in humility, seek also to grow upward—having nearer approaches to God in prayer and more intimate fellowship with Jesus.

May God the Holy Spirit enable you to "grow in the knowledge of our Lord and Saviour." He who grows not in the knowledge of Jesus, refuses to be blessed. To know him is "life eternal," and to advance in the knowledge of him is to increase in happiness.

He who does not long to know more of Christ, knows nothing of him yet. Whoever hath sipped this wine will thirst for more, for although Christ doth satisfy, yet it is such a satisfaction, that the appetite is not cloyed, but whetted. . . .

If you do not desire to know him better, then you love him not, for love always cries, "Nearer, nearer."

—CHARLES SPURGEON

PRAYER

Lord, may I ever grow nearer to You, knowing that my life is empty without You. Amen.

HOLY PRAYERS

So soon as I apply myself to prayer, I feel my whole spirit and my whole soul lift itself up without any trouble or effort of mine; and it remains as it were in elevation, fixed firm in God as in its centre and its resting-place.

—Brother Lawrence

This is reasonable as for any person to pretend to strictness in devotion, to be careful of observing times and places of prayer, and yet letting the rest of his life, his time and labour, his talents and money, be disposed of without any regard to strict rules of piety and devotion. For it is as great an absurdity to suppose holy prayers, and Divine petitions, without a holiness of life suitable to them, as to suppose a holy and Divine life without prayers.

—WILLIAM LAW

PRAYER

Lord, I lay my petitions at Your feet. Hear my prayers. Amen.

OUR GREAT TEACHER

You will see in this my Notion of Good Works, that I am far from expecting . . . that I shall merit Heaven by them. By Heaven we understand, a State of Happiness, infinite in Degree, and eternal in Duration: I can do nothing to deserve such Reward.

—Benjamin Franklin

The first thing the Lord teaches His disciples is that they must have a secret place for prayer. Everyone must have some solitary spot where he can be alone with his God. Every teacher must have a schoolroom. We have learned to know and accept Jesus as our only Teacher in the school of prayer. He has already taught us at Samaria that worship is no longer confined to specific times and places. Worship—true, spiritual worship—is a thing of the spirit and the life. A man's whole life must be worship in spirit and truth. But Jesus wants each one to choose for himself a fixed spot where he can meet Him daily. That inner chamber, that solitary place, is Jesus' schoolroom. That spot can be anywhere. It can even change from day to day if we're traveling. But that secret place must be somewhere with quiet time for the pupil to place himself in the Master's presence. Jesus comes there to prepare us to worship the Father.

—ANDREW MURRAY

PRAYER

Lord Jesus, please teach me to pray and to live a prayerful, holy life. Amen.

DAILY PRAYER FOR DAILY NEEDS

The history of liberty is a history of resistance. The history of liberty is a history of the limitation of governmental power, not the increase of it.

—Woodrow Wilson

True prayers are born of present trials and present needs. Bread for today is enough. Bread, for today, is bread enough. Bread given for today is the strongest sort of pledge that there will be bread tomorrow. Victory today, is the assurance of victory tomorrow. Our prayers need to be focused on the present. We must trust God today, and leave the morrow entirely with him. The present is ours; the future belongs to God. Prayer is the task and duty of each recurring day—daily prayer for daily needs. . . .

Today's manna is what we need; tomorrow God will see that our needs are supplied. This is the faith which God seeks to inspire.

—E. M. BOUNDS

PRAYER

Lord, thank You for meeting my needs, one day at a time. Amen.

CONFIDENT, HUMBLE PRAYER

You will think me transported with Enthusiasm, but I am not. I am well aware of the Toil and Blood and Treasure, that it will cost Us to maintain this Declaration, and support and defend these States. Yet through all the Gloom I can see the Rays of ravishing Light and Glory. I can see that the End is more than Means. And that Posterity will triumph in that day's transaction, even though we should rue it, which I trust in God we shall not.

—John Adams

Even the humblest prayer is to be prayed with confidence that God will answer. Be sure you will succeed. There is no contradiction between humility and confidence. They are in perfect harmony with each other, like repentance and faith.

This confidence is not a soothing freedom from anxiety. The saints did their best praying when they were stimulated by difficulties and driven to despair. It is precisely when they are in turbulent times that faith comes to help them. It is while they groan in the agony of some calamity that the goodness of God shines upon them. In fearful times they trust God.

It is important, then, for a believer's prayer to be the product of both feelings. . . .

God often declares that he will give to us in proportion to our faith. The logical conclusion is that we receive nothing without faith. Everything that results from prayer is obtained by faith.

—ADAPTED FROM JOHN CALVIN

PRAYER

O God, I pray that You would nurture deep faith in this country and within me. Amen.

JOHN ADAMS'S STAND FOR JUSTICE

On a cold March evening in 1770, the streets of Boston were filled with protesters. British soldiers had been stationed in the city for years to enforce unpopular taxes, and many colonists saw them as intruders. Tensions finally boiled over on March 5, outside the Custom House, where a lone British sentry was taunted by a growing crowd. Snowballs, rocks, and insults flew. Soon, more British soldiers arrived, forming a tense line as the mob pressed closer.

As tensions escalated, shots rang out. When the smoke cleared, five colonists lay dead. Outrage swept the colonies, and patriot leaders such as Samuel Adams and Paul Revere called the event a "massacre," fueling anti-British sentiment.

In the aftermath, eight soldiers and their captain were arrested and sent to trial for murder. John Adams, a respected lawyer and passionate patriot, surprised many by agreeing to defend them. Motivated by his steadfast belief in justice and the right to a fair trial, Adams saw the case as an opportunity to demonstrate that impartial law and due process should apply to all, regardless of public opinion.

Ultimately, the jury acquitted six soldiers and found two guilty of manslaughter, sparing them from death. Adams's risky decision highlighted his integrity. His defense at the Boston Massacre trial stands as a defining moment, demonstrating that justice prevailed over politics, even in revolutionary times.

PRAYER

Lord, may I stand with those who are often wronged by others. Amen.

A MIGHTY WEAPON

Every thinking man, when he thinks, realizes what a very large number of people tend to forget that the teachings of the Bible are so interwoven and entwined with our whole civic and social life that it would be literally . . . impossible for us to figure to ourselves what that life would be if these teachings were removed.

—Theodore Roosevelt

There is nothing which can so assist you to walk towards heaven with good speed, as wearing the image of Jesus on your heart to rule all its motions. It is when, by the power of the Holy Spirit, you are enabled to walk with Jesus in His very footsteps, that you are most happy, and most known to be the sons of God.

Next, for religion's sake, strive to be like Jesus. Ah! poor religion, thou hast been sorely shot at by cruel foes, but thou hast not been wounded one half so dangerously by thy foes as by thy friends. Who made those wounds in the fair hand of godliness? The professor who used the dagger of hypocrisy. The man who, with pretences, enters the fold, being nought but a wolf in sheep's clothing, worries the flock more than the lion outside. There is no weapon half so deadly as a Judas-kiss. Inconsistent professors injure the gospel more than the sneering critic or the infidel. But, especially for Christ's own sake, imitate His example.

—CHARLES SPURGEON

PRAYER

Lord, teach me how to make my prayers a mighty weapon for Your kingdom. Amen.

DON'T HOLD BACK

You do well to wish to learn . . . above all, the religion of Jesus Christ.

—George Washington

Tell God all that is in your heart, as one unloads one's heart, its pleasures and its pains, to a dear friend. Tell Him your troubles, that He may comfort you; tell Him your joys, that He may sober them; tell Him your longings, that He may purify them; tell Him your dislikes, that He may help you conquer them; talk to Him of your temptations, that He may shield you from them; show Him the wounds of your heart, that He may heal them; lay bare your indifference to good, your depraved tastes for evil, your instability. . . . Tell Him how self-love makes you unjust to others, how vanity tempts you to be insincere, how pride disguises you to yourself and others. . . .

People who have no secrets from each other never want for subjects of conversation. . . . They talk out of the abundance of the heart, without consideration they say just what they think. Blessed are they who attain to such familiar, unreserved intercourse with God!

—ADAPTED FROM FRANÇOIS FÉNELON

PRAYER

Heavenly Father, help me open myself to Your loving Spirit. Amen.

READY TO HELP

When you talk of your journey and of what you have heard and seen, you inwardly desire your own glory in all you do and say.

—John Bunyan

There is in this doctrine great encouragement to all persons to look to Christ under all manner of difficulties and afflictions, and that especially from what appeared in Christ when he was here. We have an account in the history of Christ of great numbers under a great variety of afflictions and difficulties, resorting to him for help. And we have no account of his rejecting one person who came to him in a friendly manner for help, under any difficulty whatever. But on the contrary, the history of his life is principally filled up with miracles that he wrought for the relief of such. . . . And he helped persons fully, he completely delivered them from those difficulties under which they labored. And by the doctrine of the text we learn that though he is not now upon earth, but in heaven, yet he is the same that he was then. He is as able to help, and he is as ready to help under every kind of difficulty.

—JONATHAN EDWARDS

PRAYER

Lord, I pray this country turns to You for everything that we need. Amen.

ALL GOODNESS

He who has learned to pray, has learned the greatest secret of a holy and happy life.

—William Law

O Christian! Study what love is. Study it in the word, in Christ, in God. As thou seest Him to be an ever-flowing fountain of all goodness, who has His very being and glory in this, that He lives in all that exists, and communicates to all His own blessedness and perfection as far as they are capable of it, thou wilt learn to acknowledge that he that loveth not hath not known God. And thou wilt learn, too, to admit more deeply and truly than ever before, that no effort of thy will can bring forth love; it must be given thee from above. This will become to thee one of the chief joys and beauties of the Holiest of All, that there thou canst wait on the God of love to fill thee with His love. God hath the power to shed abroad His love in our hearts, by the Holy Spirit given unto us. He has promised to give Christ, so dwelling in our heart by faith, that we shall be rooted and grounded in love, and know and have in us something of a love that passeth knowledge.

—ANDREW MURRAY

PRAYER

Father, may this country recognize You. May You dwell in our hearts forever! Amen.

PERSISTING IN PRAYER

There is no currency in this world that passes at such a premium anywhere as good Christian character.

—William McKinley

Every Christian possesses a measure of the Spirit of Christ, enough of the Holy Spirit to lead us to true consecration and inspire us with the faith that is essential to our prevalence in prayer. Let us, then, not grieve or resist Him, but accept the commission, fully consecrate ourselves with all we have, to the saving of souls as our great and our only life-work. Let us get on to the altar, with all we have and are, and lie there and persist in prayer till we receive the endowment. Now, observe, conversion to Christ is not to be confounded with the acceptance of this commission to convert the world. The first is a personal transaction between the soul and Christ relating to its own salvation. The second is the soul's acceptance of the service in which Christ proposes to employ it. Christ does not require us to make brick without straw. To whom He gives the commission He also gives the admonition and the promise. If the commission is heartily accepted, if the promise is believed, if the admonition to wait upon the Lord till our strength is renewed be complied with, we shall receive the endowment.

—CHARLES FINNEY

PRAYER
Lord, thank You for giving me the measure of faith that I need. Amen.

A STRENGTHENING PRAYER LIFE

[The Bible] is worth all the books that ever were printed.

—Patrick Henry

The sin, or the consequence of sin, that makes it impossible for God to give at once what we ask is a barrier on God's side as well as ours. The attempt to break through this power of sin . . . is what makes the striving and the conflict of prayer such a reality.

Throughout history people have prayed under a sense that there are difficulties in the heavenly world to be overcome. They plead with God for the removal of these unknown obstacles. In that persevering supplication they were brought into a state of utter brokenness and helplessness, of entire resignation to Him, of union with His will, and of faith that can take hold of Him. Then the hindrances in themselves *and* in heaven were both overcome. . . . As God prevails over us, we prevail with God.

God has so created us that the more clearly we see the reasonableness of a demand, the more readily we will surrender to it. One great reason for our negligence of prayer is that there appears to be something arbitrary . . . in the call to such persistent prayer. We need to see that this apparent difficulty is a divine necessity, and . . . it is a source of unspeakable blessing.

—ANDREW MURRAY

PRAYER

As You prevail over me, O God, I will prevail with You. Help me to submit myself to You. Amen.

A DIVINE PROVIDENCE

As long as we have unsolved problems, unfulfilled desires, and a mustard seed of faith, we have all we need for a vibrant prayer life.

—John Ortberg

In his speech "The Destiny of America," Calvin Coolidge provided insight of our Puritan forefathers.

If there be a destiny, it is of no avail to us unless we work with it. The ways of Providence will be of no advantage to us unless we proceed in the same direction. If we perceive a destiny in America, if we believe that Providence has been our guide, our own success, our own salvation requires that we should act and serve in harmony and obedience. . . .

Settlers came here from mixed motives, some for pillage and adventure, some for trade and refuge, but those who have set their imperishable mark upon our institutions came from far higher motives. . . . They were intent upon establishing a Christian commonwealth in accordance with the principle of self-government.

They were an inspired body of men. . . . They brought with them the accumulated wisdom and experience of the ages. . . .

Who can doubt that it has been guided by a Divine Providence?

PRAYER

Lord, thank You for Your guiding hand on this country. I pray that it is never removed. Amen.

STAND FAST

They that do continue to reject and slight the Word of God, they are such, for the most part, as are ordained to be damned.

—John Bunyan

"Ye are Christ's" [1 Corinthians 3:23].

You are his by donation, for the Father gave you to the Son; his by his bloody purchase, for he counted down the price for your redemption; his by dedication, for you have consecrated yourself to him; his by relation, for you are named by his name, and made one of his brethren and joint-heirs.

Labour practically to show the world that you are the servant, the friend, the bride of Jesus. When tempted to sin, reply, "I cannot do this great wickedness, for I am Christ's." Immortal principles forbid the friend of Christ to sin.

When wealth is before you to be won by sin, say that you are Christ's, and touch it not.

Are you exposed to difficulties and dangers? Stand fast in the evil day, remembering that you are Christ's.

Are you placed where others are sitting down idly, doing nothing? Rise to the work with all your powers; and when the sweat stands upon your brow, and you are tempted to loiter, cry, "No, I cannot stop, for I am Christ's."

—CHARLES SPURGEON

PRAYER

Lord, I give You my life to do with what You will! Amen.

TEACH US TO PRAY

Prayer enlarges the heart until it is capable of containing God's gift of himself.

—Mother Theresa

One day the disciples said to Jesus Christ: "Lord, teach us to pray." It was the Holy Spirit who inspired them to make this request. The Holy Spirit convinced them of their inability to pray in their own strength, and He moved their hearts to draw near to Jesus as their only Master who could teach them how they ought to pray. It was then that Jesus taught them the Lord's Prayer.

There is no Christian who is not in the same case as the disciples. . . . Ah, if we were only convinced of our ignorance and of our need of a teacher like Jesus Christ! If we would only approach Him with confidence, asking Him to teach us Himself and desiring to be taught by His grace how to converse with God!

How soon we should be skilled in it and how many of its secrets we should discover. Do not let us say that we know how to pray the prayer they learned from Him. We may know the words, but without the grace we cannot understand the meaning—and we cannot ask or receive what it expresses.

—ADAPTED FROM JEAN NICOLAS GROU

PRAYER

Lord, I am Your disciple. Teach me to pray. Amen.

THE POSSIBILITIES OF PRAYER

The patriotism that built this nation calls us to serve it in times of peace as in war.

—Clara Barton

The possibilities of prayer run parallel with the promises of God. Prayer opens an outlet for the promises, removes the hindrances in the way of their execution, puts them into working order, and secures their gracious ends. More than this, prayer like faith, obtains promises, enlarges their operation, and adds to the measure of their results. God's promises were to Abraham and to his seed, but many a barren womb, and many a minor obstacle stood in the way of the fulfilment of these promises. . . . [Prayer] removed them all, made a highway for the promises, added the facility and speediness of their realization, and by prayer the promise shone bright and perfect in its execution.

The possibilities of prayer are found in its allying itself with the purposes of God, for God's purposes and man's praying are the combination of all potent and omnipotent forces.

—E. M. BOUNDS

PRAYER

God, when I'm discouraged in prayer, remind me of the power of prayer combined with Your promises. Amen.

BROTHERLY LOVE

The whole reason why we pray is to be united into the vision and contemplation of God to whom we pray.

—Julian of Norwich

Study well the Scriptures, and get knowledge; for a knowledge of doctrine will tend very much to confirm faith. Try to understand God's Word; let it dwell in thy heart richly. When thou hast done this, "add to thy knowledge temperance." Take heed to thy body; be temperate without. Take heed to thy soul; be temperate within. Get temperance of lip, life, heart, and thought. Add to this, by God's Holy Spirit, patience; ask Him to give thee that patience which endureth affliction; which, when it is tried, shall come forth as gold.

Array yourself with patience, that you may not murmur nor be depressed in your afflictions. When that grace is won, look to godliness. Godliness is something more than religion. Make God's glory your object in life; live in His sight; dwell close to Him; seek for fellowship with Him; and thou hast "godliness;" and to that add brotherly love.

—CHARLES SPURGEON

PRAYER

Father, teach this country to pray the Scriptures so that we may draw closer to You. Amen.

REQUESTS FOR PRAYER

May He who holds in His hands the destinies of nations make you worthy of the favors He has bestowed and enable you, with pure hearts and pure hands and sleepless vigilance, to guard and defend to the end of time the great charge He has committed to your keeping.

—Andrew Jackson

When people ask you to remember someone in prayer, they will often say, "This is such a nice person!" That is like taking someone who is ill to the doctor and saying, "Make him well because he is so healthy!" Maybe what they mean by the "nice person" idea is that there may be a little hope for that individual's salvation.

Sometimes they will say, "Pray for so-and-so because this person has done good things on your behalf." I would prefer to pray for someone who has done me wrong. Such a person actually needs my prayers.

It is a good thing to pray for anyone who confesses and asks for forgiveness. It is even better to pray for someone who does not yet feel guilty about anything. Ask God to help them notice their sin. And pray also for those who know they are guilty but will not admit it. Maybe they are ashamed. Maybe they are actually enjoying their guilt. Ask God to help them.

—ADAPTED FROM GUIGO I

PRAYER

Lord Jesus, help me to be ready to love those who are difficult to love. Amen.

THE BRIGHT SIDE OF LIFE

Prayer is my chief work, by it I carry on all else.

—Attributed to William Law

Look as well on the bright side as on the dark side of the cloud; on the bright side of providence as well as on the dark side of providence. Beloved, there is a great weakness amongst Christians; they do so dwell on the dark side of the providence that they have no heart to consider the bright side. If you look on the dark side of the providence of God to Joseph, how terrible and amazing was it! but if you look on the bright side, his fourscore years' reign, how glorious was it! If you look on the dark side of the providence of God to David, in his five years' banishment, much will arise to startle you; but if you turn to the bright side, his forty years' reign in glory, how amiable was it! Look on the dark side of the providence of God to Job, oh, how terrible was it in the first of Job! but compare this with the last of Job, where you have the bright side of the cloud, and there God doubles all his mercies to him. Consider the patience of Job, and the end that the Lord made with him. Do not remember the beginning only, for that was the dark side; but turn to the end of him, and there was his bright side. Many sins, many temptations, and much affliction would be prevented by Christians looking on the bright side of providence as well as on the dark.

—THOMAS BROOKS

PRAYER

Lord, may my heart always be filled with Your light! Remove any darkness from it. Amen.

WAITING ON GOD

Never go out of your way to meet trouble. If you will just sit still, nine cases out of ten someone will intercept it before it reaches you.

—Calvin Coolidge

Those who deal with God will find it is not in vain to trust in him; for, 1. He is good to those who do so [Lamentations 3:25]. He is good to all; his tender mercies are over all his works; all his creatures taste of his goodness. But he is in a particular manner good to those that wait for him. . . .

While we wait for him by faith, we must seek him by prayer; our souls must seek him, else we do not seek so as to find. Our seeking will help to keep up our waiting. And to those who thus wait and seek God will be gracious; he will show them his marvellous lovingkindness.

2. Those that do so will find it good for them [Lamentations 3:26]. It is good . . . to hope and quietly to wait for the salvation of the Lord; to hope that it will come, though the difficulties that lie in the way of it seem insupportable, to wait till it does come, though it be long delayed, and while we wait to be quiet and silent, not quarreling with God nor making ourselves uneasy. . . .

"Father, thy will be done." If we call this to mind, we may have hope that all will end well at last.

—MATTHEW HENRY

PRAYER

Father, I know that Your will is best for me and for our nation. In all things, I pray that Your will be done. Amen.

PERSEVERING PRAYER

I doubt if there is any problem—social, political or economic—that would not melt before the fire of such a spiritual awakening.

—Franklin D. Roosevelt

Of all the mysteries of the prayer world, the need of persevering prayer is one of the greatest. That the Lord, who is so loving and longing to bless, should have to be supplicated time after time, sometimes year after year, before the answer comes, we cannot easily understand. It is also one of the greatest practical difficulties in the exercise of believing prayer. When, after persevering supplication, our prayer remains unanswered, it is often easiest for our slothful flesh, and it has all the appearance of pious submission, to think that we must now cease praying, because God may have His secret reason for withholding His answer to our request.

It is by faith alone that the difficulty is overcome. When once faith has taken its stand upon God's word, and the Name of Jesus, and has yielded itself to the leading of the Spirit to seek God's will and honour alone in its prayer, it need not be discouraged by delay. It knows from Scripture that the power of believing prayer is simply irresistible; real faith can never be disappointed.

—ANDREW MURRAY

PRAYER

Lord, sometimes the wait seems so long. Help me persevere in prayer. Amen.

FRANKLIN D. ROOSEVELT ADDRESSES THE NATION

Franklin D. Roosevelt's first inauguration occurred during the Great Depression, when America anxiously awaited his words. Roosevelt did not disappoint, offering twenty minutes of reassurance, hope, and promises for urgent action:

So, first of all, let me assert my firm belief that the only thing we have to fear is fear itself— nameless, unreasoning, unjustified terror which paralyzes needed efforts to convert retreat into advance. In every dark hour of our national life a leadership of frankness and of vigor has met with that understanding and support of the people themselves which is essential to victory. I am convinced that you will again give that support to leadership in these critical days.

A few days after his inauguration, Roosevelt began his "fireside chats," using radio to enter Americans' homes and discuss current issues. Speaking at length, unfiltered by the press, he offered a reassuring and optimistic tone often lost in print:

Confidence and courage are the essentials of success in carrying out our plan. You people must have faith. You must not be stampeded by rumors or guesses. Let us unite in banishing fear. We have provided the machinery to restore our financial system, and it is up to you to support and make it work. It is your problem, my friends, your problem no less than it is mine. Together we cannot fail.

PRAYER

Lord, I give You thanks for a country that helps others in times of need. Amen.

THE NATURE OF PRAYER

Providence has at all times been my only dependence, for all other sources seem to have failed us.

—George Washington

There are three kinds of prayer. The first is spoken prayer with a prepared text, such as the Lord's Prayer and other special prayers. It is useful to say these vocal prayers as devoutly as possible. Never say them carelessly or grudgingly. Such prayers can lift you up to God.

The second kind of prayer is spoken, but without prepared text. This is when a man or a woman feels devout and speaks to God as though they were standing together. The words match an inward stirring and reflect the various concerns of the moment. This kind of prayer pleases God. Because it comes from the heart, it never goes away without some of God's grace.

The third type of prayer is only in the heart. It is silent and brings with it great rest of body and soul. Some can pray in the heart continually, glorifying and praising God.

—ADAPTED FROM WALTER HILTON

PRAYER

Lord, may the words of my mouth make the actions of my heart. Amen.

THE GOODNESS OF GOD

The spirit of liberty that founded this nation must be extended to every soul within it.

—Attributed to Lydia Maria Child

We pray to God to know His passion, death, and resurrection—which come from the goodness of God. We pray to God for the strength that comes from his Cross—which also comes from the goodness of God. We pray to God with all the help of the saints who have gone before us—which, again, comes from the goodness of God. All of the strength that may come through prayer comes from the goodness of God, for he is the goodness of everything.

For the highest form of prayer is to the goodness of God. It comes down to us to meet our humblest needs. It gives life to our souls and makes them live and grow in grace and virtue. It is near in nature and swift in grace, for it is the same grace which our souls seek and always will.

—JULIAN OF NORWICH

PRAYER

Heavenly Father, thank You for Your goodness and grace to me and to this nation. Amen.

STOP A WANDERING MIND

Only in winter can you tell which trees are truly green. Only when the winds of adversity blow can you tell whether an individual or a country has steadfastness.

—John F. Kennedy

If your mind wanders during prayer, here is a technique that will certainly help. If you are a beginner at prayer, there is no need now for subtle meditation with many mental conceptions of Jesus. Simply look at him.

If you are in trouble or sad, look at Jesus on his way to the Garden of Gethsemane. Imagine the struggle going on inside his soul. See him bending under the weight of the cross. Look at him persecuted, suffering, and deserted by his friends.

Let your prayer begin to take shape. "Lord, if you are willing to suffer such things for me, what am I suffering for you? Why should I complain? Let me imitate your way." . . .

You ask me how you can possibly do this, protesting that Jesus is not physically present in the world today. Listen! Anyone can make the little effort it takes to look at the Lord within. You can do this without any risk and with very little bother. If you refuse to try this, it is not likely that you would have remained at the foot of the cross either.

—ADAPTED FROM SAINT TERESA OF AVILA

PRAYER

Lord God, let me be an experienced beginner in prayer. Help me to follow the guidance of those who know the way. Amen.

QUIET INSPIRATION

Thorough knowledge of the Bible is worth more than a college education.

—Theodore Roosevelt

The Scriptures say without hesitation that God's Spirit lives in us, gives us life, speaks to us in silence, inspires us, and that it is so much a part of us that we are *united* with the Lord in spirit. This is basic Christian teaching.

The Spirit of God is the soul of our soul! We are blind if we think that we are alone in the interior sanctuary. God is actually more present in this place than we are. We are constantly inspired, but we suppress the inspiration. God is always speaking to us, but the external noise of the world and the internal churning of our passions confuse us. We can't hear him speaking. Everything around us needs to be silent, and we must be quiet within. We need to focus our entire being to hear his soft whisper of a voice. The only ones who hear it are those who listen to nothing else.

—ADAPTED FROM FRANÇOIS FÉNELON

PRAYER

Lord, I am quiet right now in prayer. Before I turn away from this page, I pause to listen to You. Amen.

FAULTLESS

Jesus Christ carries on intercession for us in heaven; the Holy Ghost carries on intercession in us on earth; and we the saints have to carry on intercession for all men.

—Oswald Chambers

Do you not feel in your own soul that perfection is not in you? Does not every day teach you that? Every tear which trickles from your eye, weeps "imperfection;" every harsh word which proceeds from your lip, mutters "imperfection."

You have too frequently had a view of your own heart to dream for a moment of any perfection in yourself. But amidst this sad consciousness of imperfection, here is comfort for you—you are "perfect in Christ Jesus" [Colossians 1:28].

In God's sight, you are "complete in him;" even now you are "accepted in the Beloved." But there is a second perfection, yet to be realized, which is sure to all the seed. Is it not delightful to look forward to the time when every stain of sin shall be removed from the believer, and he shall be presented faultless before the throne, without spot, or wrinkle, or any such thing?

—CHARLES SPURGEON

PRAYER

Lord, help me always to remember that I am complete in You. Amen.

UNION IN PRAYER

Democracy is first and foremost a spiritual force. It is built upon a spiritual basis—and on a belief in God and an observance of moral principles. And in the long run only the church can provide that basis. Our founders knew this truth—and we will neglect it at our peril.

—Harry S. Truman

In this text we have an account *how* this future glorious advancement of the church of God should be introduced; *viz.* By great multitudes in different towns and countries taking up a *joint resolution*, and coming into an express and *visible agreement*, that they will, by united and extraordinary *prayer*, seek to God, that he would come and manifest himself, and grant the tokens and fruits of his gracious presence. . . .

The *good,* that shall be sought by prayer; which is God himself. It is said once and again, "They shall go to pray before the Lord, and to seek the Lord of hosts" [Zechariah 8:21]. . . . That expression of *seeking the Lord* . . . implies that *God himself* is the great *good* desired and sought after; that the blessings pursued are God's gracious presence, the blessed manifestations of him, union and intercourse with him; or, in short, God's *manifestations* and *communications* of himself by his Holy Spirit.

—JONATHAN EDWARDS

PRAYER

O Lord, I seek You and You alone, for You are the greatest good and the source of all blessings on earth. Amen.

PRAYER AND CONSECRATION

Let us have faith that right makes might, and in that faith, let us, to the end, dare to do our duty as we understand it.

—Abraham Lincoln

Prayer and consecration are closely related. Prayer leads up to, and governs consecration. Prayer is precedent to consecration, accompanies it, and is a direct result of it. . . .

Consecration is much more than a life of so-called service. It is a life of personal holiness, first of all. It is that which brings spiritual power into the heart and enlivens the entire inner man. It is a life which ever recognizes God, and a life given up to true prayer.

Full consecration is the highest type of a Christian life. It is the one divine standard of experience, of living and of service. It is the one thing at which the believer should aim. Nothing short of entire consecration must satisfy him. Never is he to be contented till he is fully, entirely the Lord's by his own consent. His praying naturally and voluntarily leads up to this one act of his.

—E. M. BOUNDS

PRAYER

Lord, there are times when my heart is not willing to be made completely Yours. Father, lead me to the place of consecration. Amen.

TIME FOR PRAYER

But to dis solemn resolution I came; I was free, and dey should be free also; I would make a home for dem in de North, and de Lord helping me, I would bring dem all dere. Oh, how I prayed den, lying all alone on de cold, damp ground; "Oh, dear Lord," I said, "I haint got no friend but you. Come to my help, Lord, for I'm in trouble!"

—Harriet Tubman

There are earnest Christians who have just enough prayer to maintain their spiritual position but not enough to grow spiritually. Seeking to fight off temptation is a defensive attitude rather than an assertive one which reaches for higher attainment. The scriptural teaching to cry out day and night in prayer must, to some degree, become our experience if we are to be intercessors.

A man said to me, "I see the importance of much prayer, and yet my life hardly allows time for it. Am I to give up? How can I accomplish what I desire?" . . .

In our communication with heaven, we only get as we give. Unless we are willing to pay the price—to sacrifice time and attention and seemingly necessary tasks for the sake of the heavenly gifts—we cannot expect much power from heaven in our work.

—ANDREW MURRAY

PRAYER

Heavenly Father, help me to remember that You are the most important thing in my life. Amen.

THE NEW COLOSSUS

The Statue of Liberty was presented to the United States by the people of France in 1886. Located in New York Harbor, it stands on Liberty Island as a symbol of freedom and a welcome to all visitors, immigrants, and returning Americans. Inside the Statue, a bronze plaque bears Emma Lazarus's famous poem "The New Colossus," which powerfully expresses the statue's meaning as a beacon of hope.

Not like the brazen giant of Greek fame,
With conquering limbs astride from land to land;
Here at our sea-washed, sunset gates shall stand
A mighty woman with a torch, whose flame
Is the imprisoned lightning, and her name
Mother of Exiles. From her beacon-hand
Glows world-wide welcome; her mild eyes command
The air-bridged harbor that twin cities frame.
"Keep, ancient lands, your storied pomp!" cries she
With silent lips. "Give me your tired, your poor,
Your huddled masses yearning to breathe free,
The wretched refuse of your teeming shore.
Send these, the homeless, tempest-tost to me,
I lift my lamp beside the golden door!"

PRAYER

Lord, let our nation always see our fellow man as someone You love! Amen.

RECOVERY

The hill, though high, I desire to ascend, The difficulty will not me offend; For I perceive.

—Patrick Henry

Take your problems promptly to God. He could help you much faster if you were not so slow in turning to prayer, but you try everything else first.

Now that you have caught your breath and your trouble has passed, recuperate in God's mercies. God is near you to repair all damage and to make things better than before. Is anything too hard for God? Where is your faith? Stand strong in God. Have patience and courage. Comfort will come in time. Wait. He will come to you with healing.

Are you anxious about the future? What will that gain you but sorrow? "Therefore do not worry about tomorrow, for tomorrow will worry about its own things. Sufficient for the day is its own trouble" (Matthew 6:34).

. . . When you think you are far from God, he is really quite near. When you feel that all is lost, sometimes the greatest gain is ready to be yours. Don't judge everything by the way you feel right now. If, for a while, you feel no comfort from God, he has not rejected you. He has set you on the road to the kingdom of heaven.

—ADAPTED FROM THOMAS À KEMPIS

PRAYER

Lord Jesus, give me strength to do Your will today. Amen.

GIVE GOD YOUR WHOLE LIFE

Give up money, give up fame, give up science, give the earth itself and all it contains rather than do an immoral act.

—**Thomas Jefferson**

Now if we conclude that we must be pious in our prayers, we must also conclude that we must be pious in all the other aspects of our lives. For there is no reason why we should make God the rule and the measure of our prayers, why we should look wholly unto Him and pray according to His will, and yet not make Him the rule and measure of all the other actions of our life. For any ways of life, any employment of our talents whether of our bodies, our time, or money that are not strictly according to the will of God, that are not done to His glory are simply absurdities, and our prayers fail because they are not according to the will of God. . . . It is our strict duty to live by reason, to devote all of the action of our lives to God. . . . If our prayers do not lead us to this, they are of no value no matter how wise or heavenly.

—ADAPTED FROM WILLIAM LAW

PRAYER

Heavenly Father, I pray this country gives itself entirety over to Your loving care. Amen.

GOD IN THE COMMONPLACE

We must be free not because we claim freedom, but because we practice it.

—William Faulkner

Here are the secrets of intimacy with God: Renounce everything that does not lead to God. Become accustomed to a continual conversation with him in freedom and simplicity. Speak to him every moment.

Ask him to tell you what to do when you are not sure. Get busy with it when you plainly see what he requires of you.

Offer your activity to him even before you do it. Give God thanks when you accomplish something.

The depth of your spirituality does not depend upon changing the things you do but in doing for God what you ordinarily do for yourself.

The biggest mistake is to think that a time of prayer is different from any other time. It is all one. Prayer is experiencing the presence of God. There should be no change when a time of formal prayer ends. Continue with God. Praise and bless him with all your energy.

—ADAPTED FROM BROTHER LAWRENCE

PRAYER

God, I pray that You will continue to be with me. Assist me. Possess all my affections. Amen.

GIVE GOD YOUR TROUBLES

Difficult roads often lead to beautiful destinations.

—Zig Ziglar

What are the things we should lay before the Almighty God in prayer? Answer: First, our personal troubles. In Psalm 32, David cried out, "Thou art my hiding place; thou shalt preserve me from trouble; thou shalt compass me about with songs of deliverance" (v. 7). Likewise, in Psalm 142, "I cried unto the Lord with my voice; with my voice unto the Lord did I make my supplication" (v. 1). When we pray, we should keep in mind all the shortcomings and excesses we feel, and pour them out freely to God, our faithful Father, who is ready to help. If you do not know or recognize your needs, or think you have none, then you are in the worst possible place. The greatest trouble we can ever know is thinking that we have no trouble for we have become hard-hearted and insensible to what is inside of us.

—ADAPTED FROM MARTIN LUTHER

PRAYER

Father, I lay all my troubles and needs before You today. Amen.

THE TURNING POINT: THE BATTLE OF SARATOGA

While we are Contending for our own Liberty, we should be very cautious of violating the rights of Conscience in others; ever considering that God alone is the Judge of the Hearts of Men, and to him only in this Case they are answerable.

—George Washington

In September 1777, British General John Burgoyne set out from Canada with a bold plan: lead his army south through New York to join other British forces and split the American colonies by taking the Hudson River Valley. Over the next several weeks, the wilderness slowed him. By October, the other British armies had not arrived, leaving Burgoyne stranded deep in enemy territory.

Meanwhile, General Horatio Gates, along with Benedict Arnold and Daniel Morgan, positioned American forces near Saratoga to counter the British advance. On September 19, at Freeman's Farm, Burgoyne launched an attack. Although the British held the field, they suffered heavy losses while American confidence grew.

Encouraged by his earlier effort, Burgoyne pressed his attack, but the Americans anticipated his move. Arnold, disregarding orders, led a bold counterattack that broke the British lines. Isolated, Burgoyne surrendered his entire force on October 17, 1777.

PRAYER

Lord, when things are difficult in our nation, give us strength to endure. Amen.

THE LIGHT OF HOPE

It is Religion and Morality alone, which can establish the Principles upon which Freedom can securely stand.

—John Adams

Come to God with all your desires and instincts, all your lofty ideals, all your longing for purity and unselfishness, all your yearning to love and be true, all your aspirations after self-forgetfulness and childlikeness; come to Him with all your weaknesses, all your shames, all your futilities; with all your helplessness over your own thoughts. . . . Be sure of this, He will take you and all your misery into His care, for liberty in His limitless heart. He is light, and in Him there is no darkness at all. If He were a king, a governor, if the name that described Him were the Almighty, you may well doubt whether there could be light enough in Him for you and your darkness. But, He is your Father, and more your Father than the word can mean in any lips but His who said, "My father and your father, my God and your God."

—ADAPTED FROM GEORGE MACDONALD

PRAYER

Father, I bring all of myself to You. Take my heart and make it Your own. Amen.

CONTINUAL PRAYER

The Almighty God . . . has given to our country a faith which has become the hope of all peoples in an anguished world.

—Franklin D. Roosevelt

What is prayer? Not the utterance of words. They are but the vehicle of prayer. Prayer is the attitude of a person's spirit, and the elements of prayer may be diffused throughout our daily lives. . . .

Our continual submission to God's will is . . . essential for all prayer. Many people believe that praying is urging our wishes on God, and answered prayer is God giving us what we desire. The deepest expression of true prayer is not, "Do this, because I desire it, O Lord." Rather, it is, "I do this because you desire it, O Lord." . . .

So there should run all through our daily lives the music of continual prayer beneath our various occupations, like some prolonged, deep, bass note that bears up and dignifies the lighter melody rising, falling, and changing above it. Then our lives can be woven into a harmonious unity based upon a continual communion, a continual desire after God, and a continual submission to Him.

—ADAPTED FROM ALEXANDER MACLAREN

PRAYER

Lord, as I remain in continual prayer, I know You will help me to follow You. Amen.

A DIFFERENCE

It is better in prayer to have a heart without words than words without heart.

—John Bunyan

What a difference it would make in the world if every believer were to give himself with his whole heart to live for his fellow men! What a difference to his own life, as he yielded himself to God's saving love in its striving for souls! What a difference to all our Christian agencies, suffering for want of devoted, whole-hearted helpers! What a difference to our churches, as they rose to know what they have been gathered for! What a difference to thousands of lost ones, who would learn with wonder what love there is in God's children, what power and blessing in that love! Let us consider one another.

—ANDREW MURRAY

PRAYER

Lord, may my prayers to You always be on my lips! And may the prayers of our nation be never ceasing. Amen.

WHEN GOD SAYS NO

There is not a truth existing which I fear, or would wish unknown to the whole world.

—**Thomas Jefferson**

Whatsoever we ask which is not for our good, He will keep it back from us. And surely in this there is no less of love than in the granting what we desire as we ought. . . . Will not the same love which prompts you to give a good, prompt you to keep back an evil, thing? If, in our blindness, not knowing what to ask, we pray for things which would turn in our hands to sorrow and death, will not our Father, out of His very love, deny us? . . . How awful would be our lot, if our wishes should straightway pass into realities; if we were endowed with a power to bring about all that we desire; if the inclinations of our will were followed by fulfillment of our hasty wishes, and sudden longings were always granted. . . .

One day we shall bless Him, not more for what He has granted than for what He has denied.

—HENRY EDWARD MANNING

PRAYER

Heavenly Father, help me remember Your goodness and mercy to me and to this country today. Amen.

PROCLAIM LIBERTY

In 1751, the Pennsylvania Assembly ordered a bell. The purpose was to commemorate the golden anniversary of William Penn's 1701 Charter of Privileges. This charter, Pennsylvania's original constitution, speaks of the rights and freedoms valued by people the world over. The biblical quotation, "Proclaim liberty throughout all the land unto all the inhabitants thereof," was particularly apt. The words immediately preceding "proclaim liberty" are, "And ye shall hallow the fiftieth year."

Decades after its creation, tradition holds that on July 8, 1776, the Liberty Bell rang from the tower of Independence Hall, calling citizens of Philadelphia to the first public reading of the Declaration of Independence. In reality, the steeple was already in disrepair by that time, leading historians today to doubt this account. Despite this, the Liberty Bell's association with the Declaration of Independence became embedded in America's memory over the years.

Years later, in 1837, abolitionists advocating for the end of slavery adopted the Liberty Bell as a symbol of emancipation and liberty. This symbolism, established decades after the bell's traditional association with independence, continues today.

PRAYER

Lord, thank You for gentle reminders of the freedom our nation gave us so many years ago. May we never forget. Amen.

THE CHIEF END OF PRAYER

Any concern too small to be turned into prayer is too small to be made into a burden.

—Corrie ten Boom

This was Jesus' goal when He was on earth: "I seek not mine own honor: I seek the honor of Him who sent me." In such words we have the keynote of His life. . . .

Let us make His aim ours! Let the glory of the Father be the link between our asking and His doing!

Jesus' words come indeed as a sharp two-edged sword, dividing the soul and the spirit, and quickly discerning the thoughts and intents of the heart. In His prayers on earth, His intercession in heaven, and His promise of an answer to our prayers, Jesus makes His first object the glory of His Father. Is this our object, too? Or are self-interest and self-will the strongest motives urging us to pray? A distinct, conscious longing for the glory of the Father must animate our prayers. . . .

For the sake of God's glory, let us learn to pray well. . . .

When we seek our own glory among men, we make faith impossible. . . . The surrender to God and the expectation that He will show His glory in hearing us are essential. Only he who seeks God's glory will see it in the answer to his prayer.

—ANDREW MURRAY

PRAYER

Lord, help me to set aside my own selfish interests and focus solely on Your will. Amen.

PRAYER AND DEVOTION

I use all the brains I have and borrow all I can from the classics and wise sayings.

—Attributed to Woodrow Wilson

The root of devotion is to devote to a sacred use. . . . Prayer promotes the spirit of devotion, while devotion is favorable to the best praying. Devotion furthers prayer and helps to drive prayer home to the object which it seeks. Prayer thrives in the atmosphere of true devotion. It is easy to pray when in the spirit of devotion. The attitude of mind and the state of heart implied in devotion make prayer effectual in reaching the throne of grace. God dwells where the spirit of devotion resides. All the graces of the Spirit are nourished and grow well in the environment created by devotion. Indeed, these graces grow nowhere else but here. . . . True worship finds congeniality in the atmosphere made by a spirit of devotion. While prayer is helpful to devotion, at the same time devotion reacts on prayer, and helps us to pray.

—E. M. BOUNDS

PRAYER

God, as I pray, I ask You to make me more wholly devoted to You. Amen.

THE PRAYER THAT TRANSFORMS

All growth depends upon activity. Life is manifest only by action. There is no development physically or intellectually without effort, and effort means work.

—Calvin Coolidge

That prayer which does not succeed in moderating our wish, in changing the passionate desire into still submission, the anxious, tumultuous expectation into silent surrender, is no true prayer, and proves that we have not the spirit of true prayer. . . .

That life is most holy in which there is least of petition and desire, and most of waiting upon God: that in which petition most often passes into thanksgiving. . . .

Pray till prayer makes you forget your own wish, and leave it or merge it in God's Will. The Divine wisdom has given us prayer, not as a means whereby to obtain the good things of earth, but as a means whereby we learn to do without them; not as a means whereby we escape evil, but as a means whereby we become strong to meet it.

—FREDERICK WILLIAM ROBERTSON

PRAYER

God, I pray for Your transforming power over this country today. Amen.

LOVE AND SALVATION

You gain strength, courage, and confidence by every experience in which you really stop to look fear in the face. . . . You must do the thing you think you cannot do.

—Eleanor Roosevelt

Will you say that you are afraid to come to God? Your fear is needless. You shall not be cast out, if you will but come in the way of faith in Christ. Our God is not "an austere man." Our Father in heaven is full of mercy, love, and grace. I yield to none in desire to exalt the love, mercy, and tenderness of God the Father. . . .

We know that God is holy. We know He is just. We believe that He is angry with those who go on still in sin. But we also believe that to those who draw near to Him in Christ Jesus, He is most merciful, most loving, most tender, and most compassionate. We tell you that the cross of Jesus Christ was the result and consequence of that love. . . .

Draw near in faith by that living way, Christ Jesus, to the Father. . . . As the father did to the prodigal son when he ran to meet him, fell on his neck and kissed him, so will God the Father do to that soul who draws near to Him in the name of Christ.

—J. C. RYLE

PRAYER

Heavenly Father, I am overwhelmed by Your love and compassion as You welcome me with open arms. Amen.

CLEANSING PRAYER

Keep us little and unknown, prized and loved by God alone.

—Charles Wesley

Prayer is the most effective means at our disposal for the cleansing of our mind and emotions. This is because it places the mind in God's bright light and the emotions in his warm love. Prayer is like water that makes plants grow and extinguishes fires.

Best of all is silent, inward prayer, especially if it reflects upon our Lord's loving sacrifice. If you think of him frequently, he will occupy your soul. You will catch on to his manner of living and thinking. You will begin to live and think like him. It is exactly like the way children learn to talk, by listening to their mothers and then making sounds with their own voices.

There is no other way. Prayer is essential. Find an hour each day, in the morning if possible, and pray.

—ADAPTED FROM SAINT FRANCIS DE SALES

PRAYER

Lord, please cleanse my heart and mind as I come to You today. Amen.

A RULE TO GO BY

God's cause is committed to men; God commits himself to men. Praying men are the deputies of God; they do his work and carry out his plans.

—E. M. Bounds

Walk by no rule but such as you dare die by and stand by in the great day of Jesus Christ. You may have many ways prescribed to worship by; but walk by none but such as you dare die by, and stand by, before Jesus Christ. Walk not by a multitude, for who dares stand by that rule when he comes to die?

Make not the example of great men a rule to go by, for who dares die by and stand by this in the great day of account. Do not make any authority that stands in opposition to the authority of Christ a rule to walk by, for who dares stand by this before Jesus Christ? Ah! sirs, walk by no rule but what you dare die by, and stand by at the great day.

—THOMAS BROOKS

PRAYER

Lord, may I live each day knowing that I stand for You and You alone! Amen.

NEWBORN BABES

Keep praying in order to get a perfect understanding of God Himself.

—Oswald Chambers

It is very observable, that there is not one command in all the Gospel for public worship; and perhaps it is a duty that is least insisted upon in Scripture of any other. The frequent attendance at it is never so much as mentioned in all the New Testament. Whereas that religion or devotion which is to govern the ordinary actions of our life is to be found in almost every verse of Scripture. Our blessed Saviour and His Apostles are wholly taken up in doctrines that relate to common life. They call us to renounce the world, and differ in every temper and way of life, from the spirit and the way of the world: to renounce all its goods, to fear none of its evils, to reject its joys, and have no value for its happiness: to be as new-born babes, that are born into a new state of things: to live as pilgrims in spiritual watching, in holy fear, and heavenly aspiring after another life: to take up our daily cross, to deny ourselves, to profess the blessedness of mourning, to seek the blessedness of poverty of spirit: to forsake the pride and vanity of riches, to take no thought for the morrow, to live in the profoundest state of humility.

—WILLIAM LAW

PRAYER

Lord, please remove all pride and vanity from my heart and from the hearts of all in this country! Amen.

THE DEBT IS PAID

Christ paid a debt he didn't owe and one we couldn't pay.

— Andy Stanley

As God's creatures, we are all debtors to him: to obey him with all our body, and soul, and strength. Having broken his commandments, as we all have, we are debtors to his justice, and we owe to him a vast amount which we are not able to pay.

But of the Christian it can be said that he does not owe God's justice anything, for Christ has paid the debt his people owed; for this reason the believer owes the more to love. I am a debtor to God's grace and forgiving mercy; but I am no debtor to his justice, for he will never accuse me of a debt already paid.

Christ said, "It is finished!" and by that he meant, that whatever his people owed was wiped away forever from the book of remembrance. Christ, to the uttermost, has satisfied divine justice; the account is settled; the handwriting is nailed to the cross; the receipt is given, and we are debtors to God's justice no longer.

But then, because we are not debtors to our Lord in that sense, we become ten times more debtors to God than we should have been otherwise.

—CHARLES SPURGEON

PRAYER

Lord, may my desires be only what You will for my life. Amen.

AN ARDENT DESIRE

Pray not for crutches but for wings!

—Phillips Brooks

Although it is true that while we are listless or insensible to our wretchedness, he wakes and watches for use and sometimes even assists us unasked; it is very much for our interest to be constantly supplicating him; first, that our heart may always be inflamed with a serious and ardent desire of seeking, loving and serving him, while we accustom ourselves to have recourse to him as a sacred anchor in every necessity; secondly, that no desires, no longing whatever, of which we are ashamed to make him the witness, may enter our minds, while we learn to place all our wishes in his sight, and thus pour out our heart before him; and, lastly, that we may be prepared to receive all his benefits with true gratitude and thanksgiving, while our prayers remind us that they proceed from his hand. Moreover, having obtained what we asked, being persuaded that he has answered our prayers, we are led to long more earnestly for his favor, and at the same tine have greater pleasure in welcoming the blessings which we perceive to have been obtained by our prayers.

—JOHN CALVIN

PRAYER

Lord, I give You thanks for the many blessings You have bestowed on me and my family. Thank You for Your graciousness! Amen.

HELP IN THE HARD TIMES

We are not weak if we make a proper use of those means which the God of nature hath placed in our power.

—Patrick Henry

Oh, the burdens that we love to bear and cannot understand! Oh, the inarticulate outreachings of our hearts for things we cannot comprehend! And yet we know they are an echo from the throne and a whisper from the heart of God. It is often a groan rather than a song, a burden rather than a buoyant wing. But it is a blessed burden, and it is a groan whose undertone is praise and unutterable joy. It is a groaning "which cannot be uttered" [Romans 8:26]. We could not ourselves express it always, and sometimes we do not understand any more than that God is praying in us, for something that needs His touch and that He understands.

And so we can just pour out the fullness of our heart, the burden of our spirit, the sorrow that crushes us, and know that He hears, He loves, He understands, He receives; and He separates from our prayer all that is imperfect, ignorant and wrong, and presents the rest, with the incense of the great High Priest, before the throne on high; and our prayer is heard, accepted, and answered in His name.

—A. B. SIMPSON

PRAYER

Lord, thank You for Your Holy Spirit who intercedes for me, even when I don't know what to pray. Amen.

PERSEVERING IN PRAYER

Energy and persistence conquer all things.

—Benjamin Franklin

One of the greatest drawbacks to the life of prayer is the fact that the answer does not come as speedily as we expect. We are discouraged by the thought: "Perhaps I do not pray right." So we do not persevere in prayer. This is a lesson that our Lord taught often and urgently. . . . There may be a reason for the delay, and the waiting may bring a blessing to our souls. Our desire must grow deeper and stronger, and we must ask with our whole heart. God puts us into the practicing school of persevering prayer, that our weak faith may be strengthened.

Above all, God would draw us into closer fellowship with Himself. When our prayers are not answered, we learn to realize that the fellowship and nearness and love of God are more to us than the answers of our petitions, and we continue in prayer. . . .

Those who have persevered often and long before God, in pleading His promises, are those who have had the greatest power with God in prayer.

—ANDREW MURRAY

PRAYER

Heavenly Father, help me to learn that spending time with You is what's important. Amen.

THE MIDNIGHT RIDERS

One if by land, and two if by sea.

—Henry Wadsworth Longfellow

On April 18, 1775, Boston's quiet streets were tense. British troops prepared to march on Lexington and Concord to seize weapons and arrest leaders. In the dark, Paul Revere, a skilled silversmith and patriot, mounted his horse. His urgent mission: to warn the countryside that the British were coming.

Guided by lantern signals from the Old North Church, Revere rode through the night, stopping at each house and shouting, "The regulars are coming out!" He wasn't alone. William Dawes took another route, and later Dr. Samuel Prescott joined, carrying the warning farther after Revere's capture. Their combined effort awakened militias across Massachusetts at dawn.

While Massachusetts stirred that April night, a year later and far to the south, another midnight ride made history. In April 1777, Sybil Ludington, just sixteen, rode nearly forty miles through a stormy New York night to rally militia against a British attack on Danbury, Connecticut. Her bravery matched—and even surpassed—her male counterparts as she warned scattered farms and villages along her route.

These midnight riders, both famous and lesser known, carried more than messages; they carried a revolution's hopes. Their courage in the darkness helped spark America's first shots for freedom.

PRAYER

Lord, give courage to me and to our nation when things seem difficult and often dark. Amen.

HEALING PRAYER

Grief drives Men into the habits of Serious Reflection, Sharpens the Understanding and softens the heart.

—John Adams

Into Simon's house illness had entered; fever in a deadly form had prostrated his mother-in-law; and as soon as Jesus came they told him of the sad affliction, and he hurried to the patient's bed.

Have you any sickness in the house this morning? You will find Jesus by far the best physician, go to him at once and tell him all about the matter. Immediately lay the case before him. It concerns one of his people, and therefore will not be trivial to him.

Observe, that at once the Saviour restored the sick woman; none can heal as he does. We may not make sure that the Lord will at once remove all disease from those we love, but we may know that believing prayer for the sick is far more likely to be followed by restoration than anything else in the world; and where this avails not, we must meekly bow to his will by whom life and death are determined.

The tender heart of Jesus waits to hear our griefs, let us pour them into his patient ear.

—CHARLES SPURGEON

PRAYER

Lord Jesus, thank You for the healing of body and spirit that comes when I pray. Amen.

THE ABSENT BRIDEGROOM

In regard to this Great Book [the Bible], I have but to say, it is the best gift God has given to man.

—Abraham Lincoln

The betrothed bride has learnt to love her Lord, and no other society than His can satisfy her. His visits may be occasional and may be brief; but they are precious times of enjoyment. Their memory is cherished in the intervals, and their repetition longed for. There is no real satisfaction in His absence, and yet, alas! He is not always with her; He comes and goes. . . . Like the ever-changing tide, her experience is an ebbing and flowing one; it may even be that unrest is the rule, satisfaction the exception. Is there no help for this? Must it always continue so? Has He, can He have created these unquenchable longings only to tantalize them? Strange indeed it would be if this were the case.

The Bridegroom is waiting for thee all the time; the conditions that debar His approach are all of thine own making. Take the right place before Him, and He will be most ready, most glad, to "Satisfy thy deepest longings, to meet, supply thine every need."

—HUDSON TAYLOR

PRAYER

O Great Bridegroom, I love to spend time in Your presence. You are my joy forever! Amen.

THE TERRITORY OF THE HEART

The most tremendous judgment of God in this world is the hardening of the hearts of men.

—John Owen

O God! We don't know who you are! "The light shineth in darkness" (John 1:5) but we don't see it. Universal light! It is only because of you that we can see anything at all. Sun of the soul! You shine more brightly than the sun in the sky. You rule over everything. All I see is you. Everything else vanishes like a shadow. The one who has never seen you has seen nothing. That person lives a make-believe life, lives a dream. . . .

But I always find you within me. You work through me in all the good I accomplish. How many times I was unable to check my emotions, resist my habits, subdue my pride, follow my reason, or stick to my plan! Without you I am "a reed shaken with the wind" (Matthew 11:7). You give me courage and everything decent that I experience. You have given me a new heart that wants nothing except what you want. I am in your hands. It is enough for me to do what you want me to do. For this purpose I was created.

—ADAPTED FROM FRANÇOIS FÉNELON

PRAYER

My Creator, thank You that in the depths of my heart, I can enjoy intimacy with You through Jesus, Your Son. Amen.

A TWO-WAY STREET

The Bible is God's chart for you to steer by, to keep you from the bottom of the sea, and to show you where the harbor is, and how to reach it without running on the rocks or bars.

—Henry Ward Beecher

The vital connection between the Word and prayer is one of the simplest and earliest lessons of the Christian life. As that newly-converted heathen put it: "I pray—I speak to my Father; I read—my Father speaks to me." Before prayer, God's Word strengthens me by giving my faith its justification and its petition. And after prayer, God's Word prepares me by revealing what the Father wants me to ask. In prayer, God's Word gives me the answer, for in it the Spirit allows me to hear the Father's voice.

Listening to God's voice is the secret of the assurance that He will listen to mine. . . . My willingness to accept His words will determine the power my words have with Him. What God's words are to me is the test of what He Himself is to me. It shows the uprightness of my desire to meet Him in prayer.

—ANDREW MURRAY

PRAYER

Father, as I pray, I ask You to speak to me through Your Word. Amen.

TALKING TO GOD

Let others say what they will of the efficacy of prayer, I believe in it, and I shall pray. Thank God! Yes, I shall always pray.

—Sojourner Truth

Our heavenly Father sends us frequent troubles to try our faith. If our faith be worth anything, it will stand the test. Gilt is afraid of fire, but gold is not; the paste gem dreads to be touched by the diamond, but the true jewel fears no test. It is a poor faith which can only trust God when friends are true, the body full of health, and the business profitable; but that is true faith which holds by the Lord's faithfulness when friends are gone, when the body is sick, when spirits are depressed, and the light of our Father's countenance is hidden. . . .

The Lord afflicts His servants to glorify Himself, for He is greatly glorified in the graces of His people, which are His own handiwork. When "tribulation worketh patience; and patience, experience; and experience, hope," the Lord is honored by these growing virtues. . . . The wisdom and power of the great Workman are discovered by the trials through which His vessels of mercy are permitted to pass. Present afflictions tend also to heighten future joy.

—CHARLES SPURGEON

PRAYER

Jesus, because of Your life and death, I can approach the Father freely. What a joy it is to come to You! Amen.

HERE ON EARTH

[Prayer] is the link between God's inexhaustible resources and people's needs . . . God is the source of power, but we are the instrument He uses to link the two together.

—Charles Stanley

With Americans fearing war against Cuba, President John F. Kennedy spoke these inspirational words in his 1961 inaugural address:

The torch has been passed to a new generation of Americans—born in this century, tempered by war, disciplined by a hard and bitter peace, proud of our ancient heritage—and unwilling to witness or permit the slow undoing of those human rights to which this nation has always been committed. . . .

Let every nation know, whether it wishes us well or ill, that we shall pay any price, bear any burden, meet any hardship, support any friend, oppose any foe to assure the survival and the success of liberty. . . .

In the long history of the world, only a few generations have been granted the role of defending freedom in its hour of maximum danger. . . . The energy, the faith, the devotion which we bring to this endeavor will light our country and all who serve it—and the glow from that fire can truly light the world.

And so, my fellow Americans: ask not what your country can do for you—ask what you can do for your country.

PRAYER

Lord, help our nation to remember what is right and what is wrong, always searching Your Word for the answers. Amen.

SECRET PRAYER

Alike for the nation and the individual, the one indispensable requisite is character.

—Theodore Roosevelt

Sometimes we need a place to come together for group prayer. . . .

But we need a secret place of prayer. This will keep us from showing off. It leaves us free to use any words we please. If we want to make gestures that increase our devotion no one else will know.

Go boldly to God. He desires your prayers and has commanded you to pray. He promises to hear you, not because you are good but because he is good.

It is false prayer that Christ condemns. The tongue and the lips are busy, the body itself may be in pain, but the heart is not talking with God. It feels no sweetness at all. It has no confidence in God's promises. . . .

There is no greater labor in the world than false prayer. When the body is compelled, and the heart unwilling, when everything is against it, then it will hurt. True prayer comforts and encourages. The body, though it were half dead, revives and is strong again. Even if many minutes pass, it seems short and easy.

—ADAPTED FROM WILLIAM TYNDALE

PRAYER

God, enlighten this country. Inform and edify us. Assure us that You know what we need even before we ask. Amen.

TEARS AND PRAYERS

No man was ever honored for what he received. Honor has been the reward for what he gave.

—Calvin Coolidge

My mother wept faithfully to you more than mothers weep for dead children. You heard her, Lord. You heard her. Nine years were to pass. All that time this faithful widow continued her weeping and mourning. She prayed every hour. But for all her efforts, you allowed me to remain in darkness.

You gave her at least two grand assurances. In a dream, you told her that you would be with me. And through a priest, you explained to her that it was pointless to try to argue me out of my errors. I was not yet ready for instruction. I was too excited by the novelty of my heresy. "Leave him alone," he told her. "Only pray to God for him. He will discover by reading how great is his error. It is not possible that the son of these tears should perish."

—ADAPTED FROM SAINT AUGUSTINE

PRAYER

Lord, thank You for those who have been faithful in prayer for me. Teach me how to be faithful in prayer for others. Amen.

PRAYER BEYOND PRAYER

May He continue to hold us close as we fill the world with our sound . . . one people under God, dedicated to the dream of freedom that He has placed in the human heart, called upon now to pass that dream on to a waiting and hopeful world.

—Ronald Reagan

It is possible, while you are praying the Lord's Prayer (or some other vocal prayer), that the Lord will give you perfect contemplation. It turns the prayer into an actual conversation with God. This works beyond our understanding. Words become unimportant. Anyone who experiences this will know that the divine Master is doing the teaching without the sound of words.

The soul is aroused to love without understanding how it loves. It understands how distinctly different this moment is from all others. This is a gift of God. It is not earned.

This is not the equivalent of mental prayer, which is silently thinking about what we are saying and to whom we are saying it.

Don't think of it as something esoteric with an unusual name. Don't let the technical term for it frighten you away.

It's like this: in regular prayer we are taking the lead with God's help. But in the perfect contemplation described above, God does everything. It is not easy to explain.

—ADAPTED FROM SAINT TERESA OF AVILA

PRAYER

Lord, right now I quiet my heart. God, be with me in the silence. Amen.

PERSISTENCE IN PRAYER

Do not anticipate trouble, or worry about what may never happen. Keep in the sunlight.

—Benjamin Franklin

Persistence has various elements—the main ones are perseverance, determination, and intensity. It begins with the refusal to readily accept denial. This develops into a determination to persevere, to spare no time or trouble, until an answer comes. This grows in intensity until the whole being is given to God in supplication. Boldness comes to lay hold of God's strength. At one time it is quiet; at another, bold. At one point it waits in patience, but at another, it claims at once what it desires. In whatever different shape, persistence always means and knows that God hears prayer; I must be heard.

—ANDREW MURRAY

PRAYER

Lord, help me to trust in You and to persevere in prayer until I receive Your answer. Amen.

GIVING ALL OF OURSELVES IN PRAYER

A churchless community where men have abandoned and scoffed at or ignored their religious needs is a community on the rapid downgrade.

—Theodore Roosevelt

Prayer has to do with the entire man. Prayer takes in man in his whole being, mind, soul and body. It takes the whole man to pray, and prayer affects the entire man in its gracious results. As the whole nature of man enters into prayer, so also all that belongs to man is the beneficiary of prayer. All of man receives benefits in prayer. The whole man must be given to God in praying. The largest results in praying come to him who gives himself, all of himself, all that belongs to himself, to God. This is the secret of full consecration, and this is a condition of successful praying, and the sort of praying which brings the largest fruits.

—E. M. BOUNDS

PRAYER

Lord God, please help me block out distractions and give You my full attention. Amen.

THE LIVING ROCK

One drop of Christ's blood is worth more than the round globe, though it were one orbicular diamond; and souls are God's jewels.

—Henry Ward Beecher

What multitudes of prayers we have put up from the first moment when we learned to pray. Our first prayer was a prayer for ourselves; we asked that God would have mercy upon us, and blot out our sin. He heard us.

But when he had blotted out our sins like a cloud, then we had more prayers for ourselves. We have had to pray for sanctifying grace, for constraining and restraining grace; we have been led to crave for a fresh assurance of faith, for the comfortable application of the promise, for deliverance in the hour of temptation, for help in the time of duty and for succor in the day of trial.

We have been compelled to go to God for our souls, as constant beggars asking for everything. Bear witness, children of God, you have never been able to get anything for your souls elsewhere. All the bread your soul has eaten has come down from heaven, and all the water of which it has drank has flowed from the living rock—Christ Jesus the Lord.

—CHARLES SPURGEON

PRAYER

Lord, pour out Your grace upon my life. May I be drenched with Your love! Amen.

COMMON CHARITY

Prayer opens the heart to God. Our prayers are the means by which our souls, though empty, are filled by God to overflowing.

—John Bunyan

If contempt of the world and heavenly affection is a necessary temper of Christians, it is necessary that this temper appear in the whole course of their lives, in their manner of using the world, because it can have no place anywhere else. If self-denial be a condition of salvation, all that would be saved must make it a part of their ordinary life. If humility be a Christian duty, then the common life of a Christian is to be a constant course of humility in all its kinds. If poverty of spirit be necessary, it must be the spirit and temper of every day of our lives. If we are to relieve the naked, the sick, and the prisoner, it must be the common charity of our lives, as far as we can render ourselves able to perform it. If we are to love our enemies, we must make our common life a visible exercise and demonstration of that love. If content and thankfulness, if the patient hearing of evil be duties to God, they are the duties of every day, and in every circumstance of our life. If we are to be wise and holy as the new-born sons of God, we can no otherwise be so, but by renouncing everything that is foolish and vain in every part of our common life.

—WILLIAM LAW

PRAYER

Lord, may this country be filled with great charity, loving others before ourselves. Amen.

KEEP ON PRAYING

The acid test of our faith in the promises of God is never found in the easy-going, comfortable ways of life, but in the great emergencies, the times of storm and of stress, the days of adversity, when all human aid fails.

—**Ethel Bell**

With a proper attitude toward God it will be easy to learn to persevere in prayer. We will discover ways to hold our own desires in check and wait patiently for the Lord. We can be sure he is always with us. We can be confident he actually hears our prayers even when the only immediate response is silence.

It is a mistake to be like impatient children who need instant gratification. There are times when God does not respond as quickly as we would like. This is not a time to be despondent. It does not mean that God is angry with you or indifferent toward you. This is certainly not the time to give up praying. Instead of being discouraged, keep on praying.

This perseverance in prayer is highly recommended to us in the Scripture. In Psalms we read how David and others became almost weary of praying. They complained that God was not responding to their prayers. But they understood that persistent faith was a requirement, and they continued to pray.

—ADAPTED FROM JOHN CALVIN

PRAYER

Lord, sometimes Your kindest answer to my plea is no— or not yet. Thank You for whatever answer You choose to give me. Amen.

WAITING ON GOD

The general Principles, upon which the Fathers Achieved Independence, were . . . the general principles of Christianity. . . .

Those general principles of Christianity, are as eternal and immutable, as the Existence and Attributes of God.

—John Adams

In praying we are often occupied with ourselves, with our own needs, and our own efforts in the presentation of them. In waiting upon God, the first thought is of *the God upon whom we wait*. . . . God longs to reveal Himself, to fill us with Himself. Waiting on God gives Him time in His own way and divine power to come to us. . . .

Before you pray, bow quietly before God, just to remember and realize who He is, how near He is, how certainly He can and will help. Just be still before Him, and allow His Holy Spirit to waken and stir up in your soul the childlike disposition of absolute dependence and confident expectation. . . . Wait on God until you know you have met Him; prayer will then become so different.

And when you are praying, let there be intervals of silence, reverent stillness of soul, in which you yield yourself to God, in case He may have aught He wishes to teach you or to work in you.

—ANDREW MURRAY

PRAYER

Lord, cleanse my mind of all selfish thoughts as I linger in Your presence and yield myself to You. Amen.

PRAY DILIGENTLY

He that falls in love with himself will have no rivals.

—Benjamin Franklin

The act of prayer teaches us our unworthiness, which is a very salutary lesson for such proud beings as we are. If God gave us favors without constraining us to pray for them, we should never know how poor we are; but a true prayer is an inventory of wants, a catalogue of necessities, a revelation of hidden poverty. While it is an application to divine wealth, it is a confession of human emptiness. The most healthy state of a Christian is to be always empty in self, and constantly depending upon the Lord for supplies; to be always poor in self, and rich in Jesus; weak as water personally, but mighty, through God, to do great exploits; and hence the use of prayer, because, while it adores God, it lays the creature where it should be, in the very dust.

Prayer is in itself, apart from the answer which it brings, a great benefit to the Christian. As the runner gains strength for the race by daily exercise, so for the great race of life we acquire energy by the hallowed labor of prayer. Prayer plumes the wings of God's young eaglets, that they may learn to mount above the clouds. Prayer girds the loins of God's warriors, and sends them forth to combat with their sinews braced and their muscles firm.

—CHARLES SPURGEON

PRAYER

God, my prayers are a mighty weapon in Your hands. As I pray with great diligence, You work on my behalf. Amen.

THE TURTLE

[Bushnell] is a Man of great Mechanical powers—fertile of invention—and a master in execution.

—George Washington

During the Revolutionary War, innovation often matched bravery. The USS *Turtle* was the first military submarine. Invented in 1775 by David Bushnell, a young Connecticut inventor, it was a bold answer to the dominant British navy.

The *Turtle* was a one-man, hand-powered wooden submersible—a vessel designed to operate underwater. Shaped like two turtle shells and about 7 1/2 feet tall, it was operated by one person. To maneuver, the *Turtle* used hand-cranked propellers—rotating blades turned by hand to move the vessel—and water pumps, devices that brought water in or out to control buoyancy and depth. Its mission was to attach a gunpowder charge to a British warship hull.

In September 1776, the *Turtle* targeted HMS *Eagle* in New York Harbor. Sergeant Ezra Lee volunteered as a pilot, and under the cover of night, he maneuvered toward the ship. However, the *Eagle*'s metal plating prevented attaching the explosive. After several failed attempts, Lee abandoned the mission.

Although the attack failed, the *Turtle* still marked a milestone in naval warfare, as it was the first recorded submarine used in combat. The craft showcased American ingenuity against overwhelming odds.

PRAYER

Lord, thank You for giving ingenuity to men and women in our nation. I ask You also to give us hearts that seek Yours. Amen.

SLEEPY IN PRAYER

If you could first know where we are, and whither we are tending, we could then better judge what to do, and how to do it.

—Abraham Lincoln

Let us pray urgently and groan with continual requests. For not long ago, I was scolded in a vision because we were sleepy in our prayers and didn't pray with watchfulness. Undoubtedly, God, who "rebukes whom He loves," rebukes in order to correct and corrects to preserve. Therefore, let us break away from the bonds of sleep and pray with urgency and watchfulness. As the Apostle Paul commands us, "Continue in prayer, and watch in the same." For the apostles continually prayed day and night. Also, the Lord Jesus Himself, our teacher and example, frequently and watchfully prayed. . . . Certainly, what He prayed for He prayed on our behalf since He wasn't a sinner but bore the sins of others. In another place we read, "And the Lord said to Peter, 'Behold, Satan has desired to sift you as wheat: but I have prayed for thee, that thy faith fail not.'" If He labored, watched, and prayed for us and our sins, we should all the more be continually in prayer. First of all, pray and plead with the Lord. Then, through Him, be restored to God the Father!

—ADAPTED FROM SAINT CYPRIAN

PRAYER

Lord, I long to be diligent in my prayers. Keep me awake and alert in You! Amen.

UNITY THROUGH PRAYER

Time and money spent in helping men to do more for themselves is far better than mere giving.

—Henry Ford

When a man prays for his fellow-man, for wife or child, mother or father, sister or brother or friend, the connection between the two is so close in God, that the blessing begged may well flow to the end of the prayer. Such a one then is, in his poor, far-off way, an advocate with the Father, like his master, Jesus Christ, The Righteous. He takes his friend into the presence with him, or if not into the presence, he leaves him with but the veil between them, and they touch through the veil.

—GEORGE MACDONALD

PRAYER

Lord God, I know that You desire unity among Your people. Today, I ask that You bring us closer together and closer to You. Amen.

FAITH AND PRAYER

That book, sir, is the rock on which the Republic rests.

—Andrew Jackson

Faith is that inward sense and act, of which prayer is the expression; . . . Because in the same manner as the freedom of grace, according to the gospel covenant, is often set forth by this, that he that believes, receives [Matthew 7:7–10]. . . .

Prayer is often plainly spoken of as the expression of faith. As it very certainly is in Romans 10:11–13. For the Scripture saith, "Whosoever believes on him, shall not be ashamed. For there is no difference between the Jew and the Greek, for the same Lord over all, is rich unto all that call upon him; for whosoever shall call on the name of the Lord shall be saved. How then shall they call on him in whom they have not believed?" Christian prayer is called the prayer of faith [James 5:15]. And believing is often mentioned as the life and soul of true prayer [1 Timothy 2:8; Hebrews 10:19, 22; James 1:5–6]. . . .

Faith in God, is expressed in praying to God. Faith in the Lord Jesus Christ, is expressed in praying to Christ, and praying in the name of Christ [John 14:13–14]. And the promises are made to asking in Christ's name, in the same manner as they are to believing in Christ.

—JONATHAN EDWARDS

PRAYER

Lord, I believe in You; help my unbelief. I trust in You to bring all Your promises to pass in my life. Amen.

EARLY ON THEIR KNEES

The foundations of our society and our Government rest so much on the teachings of the Bible that it would be difficult to support them if faith in these teachings should cease to be practically universal in our country.

—Calvin Coolidge

The men who have done the most for God in this world have been early on their knees. . . . If God is not first in our thoughts and efforts in the morning, he will be in the last place the remainder of the day.

Behind this early rising and early praying is the ardent desire which presses us into this pursuit after God. Morning listlessness is the index to a listless heart. . . . Christ longed for communion with God; and so, rising a great while before day, he would go out into the mountain to pray. . . . We might go through the list of men who have mightily impressed the world for God, and we would find them early after God.

A desire for God which cannot break the chains of sleep is a weak thing and will do but little good for God after it has indulged itself fully. The desire for God that keeps so far behind the devil and the world at the beginning of the day will never catch up.

—E. M. BOUNDS

PRAYER

O Lord, in the morning, I seek Your face. In the early hours, You will hear my prayer. Amen.

LAUS DEO

Christian religious symbols and biblical references adorn buildings in Washington, DC, a testimony to the place God has in our nation's history.

For example, the Washington Monument, completed in 1884, features Christian inscriptions. Its aluminum capstone is engraved with *Laus Deo*, meaning "Praise be to God." The stairwell walls contain blocks carved with phrases such as "Holiness to the Lord," "Search the Scriptures," and "Train up a child in the way he should go."

Similarly, at the Jefferson Memorial, a quote around the interior dome states, "I have sworn upon the altar of God, eternal hostility against every form of tyranny over the minds of man." Another panel states, "God who gave us life gave us liberty. Can the liberties of a nation be secure when we have removed a conviction that these liberties are the gift of God? Indeed I tremble for my country when I reflect that God is just, that His justice cannot sleep forever."

Continuing this theme, the Lincoln Memorial also displays profound references. To the right of the magnificent statue of Abraham Lincoln is carved his Second Inaugural Address, which mentions God fourteen times and quotes the Bible twice. To the left is the Gettysburg Address: "We here highly resolve these dead shall not have died in vain; that this nation, shall have a new birth of freedom."

PRAYER

Lord, may this country always remember the freedom You gave us. Amen.

PRAYER AND PROMISE

Many times I am forced in my prayers, first to beg of God that he would take mine heart, and set it on himself in Christ, and when it is there, that he would keep it there.

—John Bunyan

The great promises find their fulfillment along the lines of prayer. They inspire prayer, and through prayer the promises flow out to their full realization and bear their ripest fruit. . . .

God had promised through His prophets that the coming Messiah should have a forerunner. How many homes and wombs in Israel had longed for the coming to them of this great honor! How much hope was heaped on this event? Perchance Zachariah and Elizabeth were the only ones who were trying to realize by prayer this great dignity and blessing. At least we do know that the angel said to Zachariah, as he announced to him the coming of this great personage, "Thy prayer is heard." It was then that the word of the Lord as spoken by the prophets and the prayer of the old priest and his wife brought John the Baptist into the withered womb, and into the childless home of Zachariah and Elizabeth. . . .

God has never put his Spirit into the realm of a human heart which had never invoked by ardent praying the coming and indwelling of the Holy Spirit.

—E. M. BOUNDS

PRAYER

Lord, I long for a new spirit, one that is pure and worships You without restraint. Create a new heart within me. Amen.

THE SPIRIT INTERCEDES FOR US

We pray that if any, anywhere, are fearing that the cost of discipleship is too great, that they may be given to glimpse that treasure in heaven promised to all who forsake.

—Elisabeth Elliot

If our prayer reach or move Him it is because He first reached and moved us to pray. The prayer that reached heaven began there, when Christ went forth. It began when God turned to beseech us in Christ—in the appealing Lamb slain before the foundation of the world. The Spirit went out with the power and function in it to return with our soul. Our prayer is the answer to God's. . . . The whole rhythm of Christ's soul, so to say, was Godhead going out and returning on itself. And so God stirs and inspires all prayer which finds and moves Him. His love provokes our sacred forwardness. . . . All say, "I am yours if you will"; and when we will it is prayer. Any final glory of human success or destiny rises from man being God's continual creation, and destined by Him for Him. So we pray because we were made for prayer, and God draws us out by breathing Himself in.

—P. T. FORSYTH

PRAYER

Father, thank You for Your Spirit, who moves me to pray and also prays through me. I yield myself fully to You. Amen.

THE PLACE OF PRAYER

Christianity works while infidelity talks. She feeds the hungry, clothes the naked, visits and cheers the sick, and seeks the lost; while infidelity abuses her and babbles nonsense and profanity. "By their fruits ye shall know them."

—Henry Ward Beecher

When Christ had ascended to heaven, the disciples knew what their work was to be: continuing with one accord in prayer and supplication. This gave them power in heaven with God and on earth with men. Their duty was to wait united in prayer for the power of the Holy Spirit for their witness to Christ to the ends of the earth. The Church of Jesus Christ should be a praying, Spirit-filled church and a witnessing church to all the world.

As long as the Church maintained this character, it had power to conquer. Unfortunately, as it came under the influence of the world, it lost much of its supernatural strength and became unfaithful to its worldwide mission.

—ADAPTED FROM ANDREW MURRAY

PRAYER

Heavenly Father, help me, as part of Your church, to be an effective witness for You this day. Amen.

ON MEDITATION

The probability that we may fall in the struggle ought not to deter us from the support of a cause we believe to be just.

—Abraham Lincoln

Starving souls live at a distance from the mercy-seat, and become like the parched fields in times of drought. Prevalence with God in wrestling prayer is sure to make the believer strong—if not happy. The nearest place to the gate of heaven is the throne of the heavenly grace. . . .

Be much on your knees, for so Elijah drew the rain upon famished Israel's fields. There is another especial path dropping with fatness to those who walk therein: it is the secret walk of communion. Oh! the delights of fellowship with Jesus! Earth hath no words which can set forth the holy calm of a soul leaning on Jesus' bosom. Few Christians understand it: they live in the lowlands, and seldom climb to the-top of Nebo; they live in the outer court; they enter not the holy place; they take not up the privilege of priesthood. At a distance they see the sacrifice, but they sit not down with the priest to eat thereof, and to enjoy the fat of the burnt offering. But, reader, sit thou ever under the shadow of Jesus; come up to that palm tree, and take hold of the branches thereof; let thy Beloved be unto thee as the apple tree among the trees of the wood, and thou shalt be satisfied as with marrow and fatness.

—CHARLES SPURGEON

PRAYER

Lord, help this country to discover the reality of the spiritual life. Show us Your grace through the meditations You inspire in our soul. Amen.

IN SPIRIT AND IN TRUTH

If we mean to have Heroes, Statesmen and Philosophers, we should have learned women.

—Abigail Adams

You do not feel in the spirit of prayer; you have no spiritual uplift; you are simply indifferent. Give that unhappy mood no heed. You know very well what you ought to do. You ought to present yourself before God; you ought to say your prayers. Do that, and the devout attitude, the bended knees, the folded hands, the quiet and the silence, the lips busied with holy words, will induce the consciousness of the divine presence, and help you to pray in spirit and in truth.

—GEORGE HODGES

PRAYER

Lord, there are times when I don't feel like praying. During such times, help me to persist in doing what I know is right. Amen.

WOMEN OF THE REVOLUTION

No republic ever yet stood on a stable foundation without satisfying the common people.

—Mercy Otis Warren

While muskets roared and cannons thundered, women quietly shaped the American Revolution. They were the unseen backbone of the patriot cause, risking homes, families, and lives for liberty.

In cities and towns, Abigail Adams urged leaders to remember women's rights. Mercy Otis Warren wrote plays, poems, and histories that inspired rebellion and recorded the struggle.

On farms and in villages, women ran households as men marched to fight, tending livestock, planting crops, and managing vital supplies. Their roles expanded beyond the home as camp followers: women cooked, nursed soldiers, and carried water to the front. Notably, Molly Pitcher famously took up arms when her husband fell, firing cannons alongside men.

Riders like Sybil Ludington braved stormy nights to warn the militia, echoing Paul Revere. Deborah Sampson disguised herself as a soldier. Countless unnamed women spied, delivered messages, and smuggled supplies, risking their lives.

The Revolutionary War was not fought only by men. Women fought with resilience, intelligence, and courage at home and in the field, helping the dream of independence survive.

PRAYER

Father, may my life story highlight Your love and grace so that others can see You in me. Amen.

HEALING LOVE

Freedom prospers when religion is vibrant and the rule of law under God is acknowledged.

—Ronald Reagan

The God of patience, meekness, and love is the one God of my heart. The whole bent and desire of my soul is to seek for all my salvation in and through the merits and mediation of the meek, humble, patient, resigned, suffering Lamb of God. He alone has power to bring forth the blessed birth of these heavenly virtues in my soul. . . .

What a comfort is it to think that this Lamb of God, Son of the Father, light of the world, glory of heaven, and joy of angels is as near to us—is truly in the presence of us—as He is in the presence of heaven. A desire of our heart that presses toward Him, longing to catch one small spark of His heavenly nature, is as sure of finding Him, touching Him, and drawing power from Him as the woman who was healed by longing but to touch the border of His garment.

—ADAPTED FROM WILLIAM LAW

PRAYER

Dear Jesus, Your healing touch makes me whole. You are everything that I need. Amen.

AN UPRIGHT HEART

[All earthly delights] are but drops, but God is the ocean.

—Jonathan Edwards

Praying must come out of a cleansed heart and be presented and urged with the "lifting up of holy hands" [1 Timothy 2:8]. It must be fortified by a life aiming, unceasingly, to obey God, to attain conformity to the divine law, and to come into submission to the divine will.

Let it not be forgotten, that, while life is a condition of prayer, prayer is also the condition of righteous living. Prayer promotes righteous living, and is the one great aid to uprightness of heart and life.

The fruit of real praying is right living. Praying sets him who prays to the great business of "working out his salvation with fear and trembling" [Philippians 2:12]; puts him to watching his temper, conversation, and conduct; . . . gives him a high incentive to pursue his pilgrimage consistently by "shunning every evil way, and walking in the good."

—E. M. BOUNDS

PRAYER

Lord, today I ask You to continue to work in my life, molding me and shaping me. Amen.

KEEPING PRAYER ON TRACK

We must resist wandering thoughts in prayer. Raising our hands reminds us that we need to raise up our minds to God, setting aside all irrelevant thoughts.

—John Calvin

So you have difficulty with wandering thoughts in prayer! That's nothing new! You have a lot of company.

One way to remedy this is to tell God about it. Don't use a lot of fancy words or make your prayers too long. That in itself will destroy your attention. Pray like a poor, paralytic beggar before a rich man. Make it your business to keep your mind in the Presence of the Lord. If you have difficulty with that, don't fret about it. That will only make it worse. Bring your attention back to God in tranquility.

Another way to stay with a prayer is to keep your mind from wandering too far at other times of the day. Keep it strictly in the Presence of God. If you think of him a lot, you will find it easy to keep your mind calm in the time of prayer.

—ADAPTED FROM BROTHER LAWRENCE

PRAYER

O Lord, open the eyes of this country so that we may see You here with us. Amen.

WE ALL NEED PRAYER

I have lived, Sir, a long time, and the longer I live, the more convincing proofs I see of this truth—that God Governs in the affairs of men.

—Benjamin Franklin

You may complain that you have little interest in prayer, that it bores you, that your mind wanders when you attempt to pray. It may be more difficult for those who are engaged in business to pray and meditate than for those who live in monasteries, but it is also far more necessary. Take some time out to be with God. Notice how Jesus invited his disciples to a mountain retreat after they had returned from witnessing for him in the cities. If we live and work in a busy place where people talk and behave as though there were no God, it is all the more important that we return to him and restore our faith and love. If he who was without sin prayed without ceasing, how much more should poor sinners like us work at it?

When you pray, ask for what you will with firm faith. If you are not confident when you pray, little will come of it. God loves the heart that trusts in him. He will never ignore those who place their complete trust in him. It is like a father listening to his child.

—FRANÇOIS FÉNELON

PRAYER

Lord God, increase the faith of this great nation, and help us seek You through prayer. Amen.

THE WORD AND PRAYER

The soul can do without everything except the word of God, without which none at all of its wants are provided for.

—Martin Luther

Prayer and the Word of God are inseparable and should always go together. . . . *In His Word God speaks to me, and in prayer I speak to God.* If there is to be true conversation, God and I must both take part. If I simply pray without using God's Word, I am apt to use my own words and thoughts. What really gives prayer power is that I take God's thoughts from His Word and present them before Him. . . .

It is through the Word that the Holy Spirit gives me right thoughts of Him. The Word will also teach me how wretched and sinful I am. It reveals to me all the wonders God will do for me and the strength He will give me to do His will. The Word teaches me how to pray—with a strong desire, a firm faith, and with constant perseverance. The Word teaches me not only what I am, but what I may become through God's grace. And above all, it reminds me each day that Christ is the great intercessor, and allows me to pray in His name.

. . . Learn this great lesson, *to renew your strength each day in God's Word, and so pray according to His will.*

—ANDREW MURRAY

PRAYER

O Lord, as I learn Your Word, You teach me how to pray. Please guide me now as I seek to pray from Your Word. Amen.

HEROIC SERVANTS

Never forget that God is far more interested in our getting to know the Deliverer than simply being delivered.

—Beth Moore

President Franklin D. Roosevelt read this prayer, originally entitled "Let Our Hearts Be Stout," over the radio to an anxious nation as Allied troops invaded Nazi-occupied Europe on D-Day, June 6, 1944.

Almighty God: our sons, pride of our Nation, this day have set upon a mighty endeavor, a struggle to preserve our Republic, our religion, and our civilization, and to set free a suffering humanity. Lead them straight and true; give strength to their arms, stoutness to their hearts, steadfastness in their faith.

They will need Thy blessings. Their road will be long and hard. For the enemy is strong. . . . We know that by Thy grace, and by the righteousness of our cause, our sons will triumph. . . .

They fight to liberate. They fight to let justice arise and tolerance and good will among all Thy people. They yearn but for the end of battle, for their return to the haven of home. Some will never return. Embrace these, Father, and receive them, Thy heroic servants, into Thy kingdom. . . .

Lead us to the saving of our country, and with our sister Nations into a world unity that will spell a sure peace.

PRAYER

Lord, I give you thanks for those who came before me and gave their all to this country. Amen.

OUR NEED FOR PRAYER

We need to encourage new believers to feed on God's Word—it is nourishment for the soul.

—Billy Graham

There is no better mirror in which to see your need than the Ten Commandments. In them you will find what you lack and what you should seek. You may find in them that you have a weak faith, small hope, and little love toward God.

You may see that you do not praise and honor God as much as you praise and honor yourself. You may see that you do not love the Lord, your God, with all of your heart. When you see these things you should lay them before God, cry out to him and ask for help, and with all confidence expect help, believing that you are heard and that you will obtain mercy. . . . It is important when we have a need to go to God in prayer. I know, whenever I have prayed earnestly, that I have been heard and have obtained more than I prayed for. God sometimes delays, but he always comes.

—ADAPTED FROM MARTIN LUTHER

PRAYER

God, I do not always love You as I should. Thank You for tolerating my weakness, and increase my love for You. Amen.

YOU MUST ASK

The men who have guided the destiny of the United States have found the strength for their tasks by going to their knees. This private unity of public men and their God is an enduring source of reassurance for the people of America.

—Lyndon B. Johnson

This divine teacher of prayer lays himself out to make it clear and strong that God answers prayer, assuredly, certainly, inevitably; that it is the duty of the child to ask, and to press, and that the Father is obliged to answer, and to give for the asking. In Christ's teaching, prayer is no sterile, vain performance, not a mere rite, a form, but a request for an answer, a plea to gain, the seeking of a great good from God. It is a lesson of getting that for which we ask, of finding that for which we seek, and of entering the door at which we knock.

A notable occasion we have as Jesus comes down from the Mount of Transfiguration. He finds his disciples defeated, humiliated, and confused in the presence of their enemies . . . Their faith had not been cultured by prayer. They failed in prayer before they failed in ability to do their work. They failed in faith because they had failed in prayer. That one thing which was necessary to do God's work was prayer. The work which God sends us to do cannot be done without prayer.

—E. M. BOUNDS

PRAYER

Divine Teacher, instruct me in Your will as I spend time with You in prayer. Amen.

HE WILL ANSWER

Good deeds are such things that no man is saved for them, nor without them.

—Thomas Adams

If it looks as if he did not hear you: never mind; he does; it must be that he does; go on as the woman did; you too will be heard. She is heard at last, and in virtue of her much going; God hears at once, and will avenge speedily. The unrighteous judge cared nothing for the woman; those who cry to God are his own chosen—plain in the fact that they cry to him. He has made and appointed them to cry: they do cry: will he not hear them? They exist that they may pray; he has chosen them that they may choose him; he has called them that they may call him—that there may be such communion, such interchange as belongs to their being and the being of their Father. The gulf of indifference lay between the poor woman and the unjust judge; God and those who seek his help, are closer than two hands clasped hard in love: he will avenge them speedily.

—GEORGE MACDONALD

PRAYER

Lord, sometimes I wonder if You hear me when I pray. Help me to have faith that You will answer in Your perfect time. Amen.

ASKING WITH HOPE

The highest, the transcendent glory of the American Revolution is this—it connected in one indissoluble bond, the principles of civil government with the precepts of Christianity.

—John Quincy Adams

Blessed Jesus! It is You who has unlocked to Your people the gates of prayer. Without You, they must have been shut forever. It was Your *atoning merit* on earth that first opened them; it is Your *intercessory work* in Heaven that keeps them open still.

How unlimited the promise—"Whatever you ask!" It is the pledge of all that the needy sinner requires. . . . He seems to say to His faithful servants, "Take your request, and under this, My superscription, write what you please." He further endorses each petition with the words, "I *will* do it!" . . .

Reader, do you know the blessedness of confiding your every need and every care—your every sorrow and every cross—into the ear of the Savior? He is the "Wonderful Counselor." With an exquisitely tender sympathy, He can enter into the innermost depths of your need. That need may be great—but the everlasting arms are underneath it all.

—JOHN ROSS MACDUFF

PRAYER

Jesus, thank You for Your promise that when I ask in Your name, You will answer my prayer. Amen.

OUR GRACIOUS GOD

Remember: He wants your fellowship, and He has done everything possible to make it a reality. He has forgiven your sins, at the cost of His own dear Son. He has given you His Word, and the priceless privilege of prayer and worship.

—Billy Graham

Founding father and one of the three authors of the Federalist Papers, Alexander Hamilton wrote this concerning the nature of liberty:

The fundamental source of all your errors, sophisms and false reasonings is a total ignorance of the natural rights of mankind. Were you once to become acquainted with these, you could never entertain a thought that all men are not, by nature, entitled to a parity of privileges. You would be convinced, that natural liberty is a gift of the beneficent Creator to the whole human race, and that civil liberty is founded in that; and cannot be wrested from any people, without the most manifest violation of justice.

PRAYER

Heavenly Father, You are the giver of all good gifts. Thank You for this country and for giving us freedom to worship You.

NO PRAYER GOES WASTED

We could never learn to be brave and patient, if there were only joy in the world.

—Helen Keller

Amazing things start happening when we start praying. Prayer time is never wasted time. . . .

John Bunyan once observed, "The best prayers have often more groans than words." I experienced this kind of prayer when I had many pressing needs all around me. Honestly, I reached a point where I could hardly pray about my needs because they were so many. The only prayer I could manage was, "Help!" and I remember passionately praying it to God over thirty times until I experienced a breakthrough. Psalms declares, "O Lord, attend unto my cry" (17:1). . . . When you take one step toward God, God will take more steps toward you than you could ever count. He moved to meet my needs.

—JOHN L. MASON

PRAYER

Lord, sometimes I'm so overwhelmed I don't know how to pray. Thank You for knowing my needs and answering me when I turn to You. Amen.

THE DANGER OF PRAYERLESSNESS

Labor to keep alive in your breast that little spark of celestial fire, called conscience.

—**George Washington**

PRAYER

Lord, I pray that this country will have a strong and vibrant prayer life. I commit to persevering in prayer, with Your help. Amen.

At a subsequent meeting the opportunity was given for testimony as to what might be the sins which made the life of the Church so feeble. Some began to mention failings that they had seen in other ministers, either in conduct, or in doctrine, or in service. It was soon felt that this was not the right way; each must acknowledge that in which he himself was guilty.

The Lord graciously so ordered it that we were gradually led to the sin of prayerlessness as one of the deepest roots of the evil. No one could plead himself free from this. Nothing so reveals the defective spiritual life in minister and congregation as the lack of believing and unceasing prayer. Prayer is in very deed the pulse of the spiritual life. It is the great means of bringing to minister and people the blessing and power of heaven. Persevering and believing prayer means a strong and an abundant life.

—ANDREW MURRAY

PRAYER FUEL

Our abundant plains and mountains would yield little if it were not for the applied skill and energy of Americans working together, as fellow citizens bound up in common destiny. The achievement of brotherhood is the crowning objective of our society.

—Dwight D. Eisenhower

The Word of God is a great help in prayer. If it is lodged and written in our hearts, it will form an outflowing current of prayer, full and irresistible. Promises, stored in the heart, are to be the fuel from which prayer receives life and warmth, just as the coal, stored in the earth, ministers to our comfort on stormy days and wintry nights. The Word of God is the food, by which prayer is nourished and made strong. Prayer, like man, cannot live by bread alone, "but by every word which proceedeth out of the mouth of [God]" [Matthew 4:4].

Unless the vital forces of prayer are supplied by God's Word, prayer, though earnest even vociferous in its urgency, is in reality flabby, vapid, and void.

—E. M. BOUNDS

PRAYER

Lord, may Your words fuel my prayer and my devotion to You. Amen.

PRAYER AND PATIENCE

Human kindness has never weakened the stamina or softened the fiber of a free people. A nation does not have to be cruel in order to be tough.

—Franklin D. Roosevelt

Praise should always follow answered prayer, as the mist of earth's gratitude rises when the sun of heaven's love warms the ground. Hath the Lord been gracious to thee, and inclined His ear to the voice of thy supplication? Then praise Him as long as thou livest. Let the ripe fruit drop upon the fertile soil from which it drew its life. Deny not a song to Him who hath answered thy prayer and given thee the desire of thy heart. To be silent over God's mercies is to incur the guilt of ingratitude; it is to act as basely as the nine lepers, who, after they had been cured of their leprosy, returned not to give thanks unto the healing Lord. To forget to praise God is to refuse to benefit ourselves; for praise, like prayer, is one great means of promoting the growth of the spiritual life. . . .

Praise is the most heavenly of Christian duties. The angels pray not, but they cease not to praise both day and night; and the redeemed, clothed in white robes, with palm-branches in their hands, are never weary of singing the new song.

—SAINT FRANCIS DE SALES

PRAYER

Lord God, I surrender my heart to You today and ask You to perfect patience in me. Amen.

LET FREEDOM RING!

Prayer does change things, all kinds of things. But the most important thing it changes is us.

—R.C. Sproul

Samuel Francis Smith wrote "My Country, 'Tis of Thee," also known as "America," in 1831 while at Andover Theological Seminary. Set to a popular international melody, it soon became a favorite and served as the national anthem in the nineteenth-century United States:

My country, 'tis of thee, sweet land of liberty, of thee I sing:
Land where my fathers died, land of the pilgrims' pride,
From every mountainside let freedom ring!
My native country, thee, land of the noble free, thy name I love;
I love thy rocks and rills, thy woods and templed hills;
My heart with rapture thrills, like that above.
Let music swell the breeze, and ring from all the trees sweet freedom's song:
Let mortal tongues awake; let all that breathe partake;
Let rocks their silence break, the sound prolong.
Our fathers' God, to Thee, Author of liberty, to Thee we sing:
Long may our land be bright with freedom's holy light.
Protect us by Thy might, great God, our King.

PRAYER

Lord, thank You for the freedom we have in this country. I sing these words of praise to You today! Amen.

THE BURDEN OF SELF

Give me the Love that leads the way; The Faith that nothing can dismay; The Hope no disappointments tire; The Passion that'll burn like fire; Let me not sink to be a clod; Make me Thy fuel, Flame of God.

—Amy Carmichael

The greatest burden we have to carry in life is self. The most difficult thing we have to manage is self. Our own daily living, our frames and feelings, our especial weaknesses and temptations, and our peculiar temperaments, our inward affairs of every kind, these are the things that perplex and worry us more than anything else, and that bring us oftenest into bondage and darkness. In laying off your burdens, therefore, the first one you must get rid of is yourself. You must hand yourself and all your inward experiences, your temptations, your temperament, your frames and feelings, all over into the care and keeping of your God, and leave them there. He made you, and therefore He understands you and knows how to manage you, and you must trust Him to do it.

—HANNAH WHITALL SMITH

PRAYER

Heavenly Father, I turn all of myself over to Your care. You are my Creator, and I trust You to know what is best for me. Amen.

HOPE IN HIM

Character, my friends, is a by-product: it is produced in the great manufacture of daily duty.

—Woodrow Wilson

What a mass of hideous sickness must have thrust itself under the eye of Jesus! Yet we read not that he was disgusted, but patiently waited on every case.

What a singular variety of evils must have met at his feet! What sickening ulcers and putrefying sores! Yet he was ready for every new shape of the monster evil, and was victor over it in every form. . . .

It is even so [today]. Whatever my own case may be, the beloved Physician can heal me; and whatever may be the state of others whom I may remember at this moment in prayer, I may have hope in Jesus that he will be able to heal them of their sins.

My child, my friend, my dearest one, I can have hope for each, for all, when I remember the healing power of my Lord; and on my own account, however severe my struggle with sins and infirmities, I may yet be of good cheer.

He who on earth walked the hospitals, still dispenses his grace, and works wonders among the sons of men: let me go to him at once in right earnest.

—CHARLES SPURGEON

PRAYER

Jesus, I take hope in Your love and power to heal me and the loved ones I entrust to Your care. Amen.

ANSWERED PRAYER

We will have our rights. We say no longer by your leave. We have besought, argued and convinced, but we have failed; and we will not fail.

—Victoria Woodhull

Let me tell you how God answered the prayers of my dear mother for my conversion. . . .

She arose from the table where she was dining with an intense yearning for the conversion of her boy. She went to her room and turned the key in the door, resolving not to leave that spot until her prayers were answered. . . .

I, in the meantime, had been led to take up a little tract and while reading it was struck with the sentence, "The finished work of Christ." Immediately the words "It is finished" suggested themselves to my mind. What was finished?

Then it came to my mind, "If the whole work of salvation was finished and the whole debt paid, what is there left for me to do?" With this dawned the joyful conviction, as light flashed into my soul by the Holy Spirit, that there was nothing in the world to be done but to fall down on one's knees and, accepting this Savior and His salvation, to praise Him forevermore. Thus while my dear mother was praising God on her knees in her chamber, I was praising him in the old warehouse. . . .

—ADAPTED FROM HUDSON TAYLOR

PRAYER

Lord, I lift before You those in this great nation who do not know You. By Your Holy Spirit, draw them to Yourself. Amen.

NEVER CEASING

The man that seeks the everlasting prize; It shows you whence he comes, wither he goes. What he leaves undone; also what he does. It also shows you how he runs and runs. Till he unto the gate of glory comes.

—John Bunyan

To talk a lot in prayer is to cheapen and overuse our words while asking for something necessary. But to prolong prayer is to have our hearts throb with continual pious emotions toward the One we pray to. In most cases, prayer consists more of groaning than of speaking, of tears rather than words. He sees our tears. Our groaning isn't hidden from Him. For He made everything by a word and doesn't need human words.

—ADAPTED FROM SAINT AUGUSTINE

PRAYER

Lord, help me to open my heart fully to You, expressing joy and sorrow, laughter and pain. Thank You for hearing every prayer I pray. Amen.

JOHN F. KENNEDY'S "WE CHOOSE TO GO TO THE MOON" SPEECH

September 12, 1962

During the Cold War, the United States and USSR prioritized spaceflight for national security. The world was surprised and alarmed when the Soviet Union launched the first artificial satellite in 1957 and sent the first human into space in 1961, asserting its technological advantages. In response, John F. Kennedy urged America to put a man on the moon. In his uplifting speech at Rice University, he celebrated the country's technological advances and his administration's resolve to extend the pioneering spirit into space:

We choose to go to the moon. We choose to go to the moon in this decade and do the other things, not because they are easy, but because they are hard, because that goal will serve to organize and measure the best of our energies and skills, because that challenge is one that we are willing to accept, one we are unwilling to postpone, and one which we intend to win, and the others, too.

PRAYER

Heavenly Father, may this country always look to You for our future. Amen.

A DARING PRAYER

Dost thou love life? Then do not squander Time, for that's the Stuff Life is made of.

—Benjamin Franklin

I had some fun with God today! I dared to complain to him. I said: Explain to me, please, why you keep me in this miserable life. Why do I have to put up with it? Everything here interferes with my enjoyment of you. I have to eat and sleep and work and talk with everyone. I do it all for the love of you, but it torments me.

And how is it that when there is a little break and I can have some time with you, you hide from me? . . . I honestly believe, Lord, that if it were possible for me to hide from you the way you hide from me, you would not allow it. But you are with me and see me always. Stop this, Lord! It hurts me because I love you so much.

I said these and other things to God. Sometimes love becomes foolish and doesn't make a lot of sense. The Lord puts up with it. May so good a king be praised! We wouldn't dare say these things to earthly kings!

—ADAPTED FROM SAINT TERESA OF AVILA

PRAYER

Lord, help me to be straightforward with You rather than try to pray pretty little prayers with little life in them. Amen.

PRAY AS HE PRAYED

Above all, we must realize that no arsenal or no weapon in the arsenals of the world is so formidable as the will and moral courage of free men and women.

—Ronald Reagan

Christ's life and work, His suffering and death—it was all prayer, all dependence on God, trust in God, receiving from God, surrender to God. Thy redemption, O believer, is a redemption wrought out by prayer and intercession: thy Christ is a praying Christ: the life He lived for thee, the life He lives in thee, is a praying life, that delights to wait on God and receive all from Him. To pray in His Name is to pray as He prayed. Christ is our only example because He is our Head, our Saviour, and our Life. In virtue of His Deity and of His Spirit He can live in us: we can pray in His Name, because we abide in Him and He in us.

—ANDREW MURRAY

PRAYER

O Christ, abide in my heart as I learn to pray for Your will. Amen.

THE GREATEST THING WE CAN DO

Eternal vigilance is the price of liberty, and it does seem to me that notwithstanding all these social agencies and activities there is not that vigilance which should be exercised in the preservation of our rights.

—**Ida B. Wells**

More time and early hours for prayer would act like magic to revive and invigorate many a decayed spiritual life. More time and early hours for prayer would be manifest in holy living. A holy life would not be so rare or so difficult a thing if our devotions were not so short and hurried. A Christlike temper in its sweet and passionless fragrance would not be so alien and hopeless a heritage if our closet stay were lengthened and intensified. . . .

To pray is the greatest thing we can do: and to do it well there must be calmness, time, and deliberation; otherwise it is degraded into the littlest and meanest of things. True praying has the largest results for good; and poor praying, the least. We cannot do too much of real praying; we cannot do too little of the sham. We must learn anew the worth of prayer, enter anew the school of prayer. . . . We must demand and hold with iron grasp the best hours of the day for God and prayer, or there will be no praying worth the name.

—E. M. BOUNDS

PRAYER

Lord, I know that praying is the greatest thing I can do, but sometimes distractions keep me from You. Help me to give You the very best of my day. Amen.

THE LIMITS OF PRAYER

Let us at all times remember that all American citizens are brothers of a common country, and should dwell together in bonds of fraternal feeling.

—Abraham Lincoln

Our prayers are to be confined to what God permits. Although he invites us to "pour out [our] hearts to him" (Psalm 62:8), God does not extend it carte blanche. He does not give us a limitless range of foolish and depraved ideas. When he promises to give us what we wish, this does not include nonsense and caprice.

It happens all the time. Many pray to God about frivolous things. They have neither modesty nor reverence. They are so crass that they stupidly bring their follies to God when they would blush to tell someone else what they were thinking about. . . .

The solution to all this is for our heart to gain the same affection for God as our mind has. To help us with this, God's Spirit guides our prayers. He can tell us what is right. He can regulate our desires. Likewise the Spirit also helpeth our infirmities: for we know not what we should pray for as we ought: but the Spirit itself maketh intercession for us with groanings which cannot be uttered. God stimulates good prayer. Correct prayer is a gift from God.

—ADAPTED FROM JOHN CALVIN

PRAYER

O Lord, help me to pray as You would have me to pray. Amen.

PRAYER FOR THE SPIRIT

We have to pray with our eyes on God, not on the difficulties.

—Oswald Chambers

The Scriptures not only direct and encourage us to pray for the Holy Spirit above all things else, but it is the expressly revealed will of God that His church should be very much in prayer for that glorious outpouring of the Spirit that is to be in the latter days, and the things that shall be accomplished by it. God, speaking of that blessed event, says, "I will also let the house of Israel inquire of Me to do this for them" (Ezekiel 36:37 NKJV). . . . This doubtless implies that it is the will of God that extraordinary prayer for this mercy should precede the bestowing of it. . . . And how loud is this call to the church of God to be fervent and incessant in their cries to Him for this great mercy! How wonderful are the words to be used, concerning the manner in which such worms of the dust should address the high and lofty One who inhabits eternity! And what encouragement is here to approach the mercy seat with the greatest freedom, boldness, earnestness, constancy, and full assurance of faith, to seek from God the greatest thing that can be sought in Christian prayer.

—ADAPTED FROM JONATHAN EDWARDS

PRAYER

Heavenly Father, thank You for the gift of Your Holy Spirit, the greatest gift I could ever receive. Amen.

AMERICA! AMERICA!

Katharine Lee Bates, professor, poet, and writer of "America the Beautiful," found inspiration for this beloved hymn atop Pikes Peak, Colorado, reflecting that, "All the wonder of America seemed displayed there, with the sea-like expanse."

O beautiful for spacious skies,
For amber waves of grain,
For purple mountain majesties
Above the fruited plain!
America! America!
God shed His grace on thee,
And crown thy good with
brotherhood
From sea to shining sea!
O beautiful for pilgrim feet
Whose stern impassion'd stress
A thoroughfare for freedom beat
Across the wilderness.
America! America!
God mend thine ev'ry flaw,
Confirm thy soul in self-control,
Thy liberty in law.
O beautiful for heroes prov'd
In liberating strife,
Who more than self their country
loved,
And mercy more than life.
America! America!
May God thy gold refine
Till all success be nobleness,
And ev'ry gain divine.
O beautiful for patriot dream
That sees beyond the years
Thine alabaster cities gleam
Undimmed by human tears.
America! America!
God shed His grace on thee,
And crown thy good with
brotherhood
From sea to shining sea.

PRAYER

Lord, what a beautiful country You have given us. For this and for all You've given to us, I give You thanks! Amen.

FILLING AN EMPTINESS

He who kneels the most, stands the best.

—D. L. Moody

Lord, you began to perfect your apostles by taking away from them the very thing they didn't think they could do without—the actual presence of Jesus. . . . Once Christ was gone, you sent the Holy Spirit. . . .

But Lord, why isn't my life filled with this Spirit? It ought to be the soul of my soul, but it isn't. I feel nothing. I see nothing. I am both physically and spiritually lazy. My feeble will is torn between you and a thousand meaningless pleasures. Where is your Spirit? Will it ever arrive and "create in me a clean heart, O God" (Psalm 51:10)? Now I understand! Your Holy Spirit desires to live in an impoverished soul.

Come, Holy Spirit! There is no place emptier than my heart.

The Holy Spirit floods the soul with light, recalling in our memory the things Jesus taught when he was on earth. We find strength and inspiration. We become one with Truth.

—FRANÇOIS FÉNELON

PRAYER

Lord, glorify Yourself in me. Please breathe Your Holy Spirit in me. Amen.

SET YOUR SIGHTS HIGH

If there is one word that describes our form of society in America, it may be the word "voluntary."

—Lyndon B. Johnson

When Jesus told us to love God with all our heart, soul, and mind, he gave us a challenging task, impossible for any of us earthlings to accomplish. Nevertheless, our Lord did tell us to love this way. His purpose (as Saint Bernard pointed out) is that we should admit our weakness and seek mercy.

Faith untried may be true faith, but it is sure to be little faith, and it is likely to remain dwarfish so long as it is without trials. Faith never prospers so well as when all things are against her; tempests are her trainers, and lightnings are her illuminators. When a calm reigns on the sea, spread the sails as you will, the ship moves not to its harbor; for, on a slumbering ocean, the keel sleeps too. Let the winds rush howling forth, and let the waters lift up themselves, then, though the vessel may rock, and her deck may be washed with waves, and her mast may creak under the pressure of the full and swelling sail, it is then that she makes headway towards her desired haven. No flowers wear so lovely a blue as those which grow at the foot of the frozen glacier; no stars gleam so brightly as those which glisten in the polar sky; no water tastes so sweet as that which springs amid the desert sand; and no faith is so precious as that which lives and triumphs in adversity.

—CHARLES SPURGEON

PRAYER

Lord, give me the patience to practice prayer. Assure me that You are listening even when I stammer in my soul. Amen.

YOUR FATHER WAITS FOR YOU

America is the only nation in the world that is founded on a creed. That creed is set forth with dogmatic and even theological lucidity in the Declaration of Independence.

—**G. K. Chesterton**

Christians often complain that private prayer is not what it should be. They feel weak and sinful. Their heart is cold and dark. It is as if they have so little to pray, and in that little, no faith or joy. They are discouraged and kept from prayer by the thought that they cannot come to the Father as they ought or as they wish.

Child of God, listen to your teacher, Jesus! He tells you that when you go to private prayer, your first thought must be this: "The Father is in secret, and the Father waits for me there." . . . Get yourself into the presence of the loving Father. "As a father has compassion on his children, so the Lord has compassion on those who fear him" (Psalm 103:13 CSB). . . . Just place yourself before God and look up into God's face. Think of God's wonderful, tender, compassionate love. Just tell God how sinful and cold and dark all is. It is the Father's loving heart that will give light and warmth to yours.

—ADAPTED FROM ANDREW MURRAY

PRAYER

Heavenly Father, thank You for being a loving Father who longs to meet all my needs. Amen.

HABITUAL SENSE OF GOD

Blessed are those who can give without remembering and take without forgetting.

—Elizabeth Bibesco

Having found in many books different methods of going to God, various practices of the spiritual life, I reckoned that so much instruction only puzzled me. Simply put, all I was looking for was how to become wholly God's.

This made me resolve to give my all for His all. So, after giving myself wholly to God—that is, making satisfaction for sins by renouncing them—I renounced them for the love of Him, and I began to live as if there were none but Him and I in the world.

Sometimes I considered myself before Him as a poor criminal at the feet of his judge; at other times I beheld Him in my heart as my Father, as my God. I worshiped Him the oftenest I could, keeping my mind in His holy presence and recalling it as often as I found it wandered from Him. I found no small pain in this exercise, and yet I continued it. I made this my business, as much as all the daylong as at the appointed times of prayer. I drove away from my mind everything that was capable of interrupting my thoughts of God.

—ADAPTED FROM BROTHER LAWRENCE

PRAYER

Heavenly Father, I want to live in a state of constant communion with You. I give myself completely to You and Your will. Amen.

PRAYER, OBEDIENCE, AND FAITH

The time has come to turn to God and reassert our trust in Him for the healing of America. Our country is in need of and ready for a spiritual renewal.

—Ronald Reagan

Our days are few, and are far better spent in doing good than in disputing over matters which are, at best, of minor importance. . . . Questions upon points wherein Scripture is silent; upon mysteries which belong to God alone; upon prophecies of doubtful interpretation; and upon mere modes of observing human ceremonials, are all foolish, and wise men avoid them. Our business is neither to ask nor answer foolish questions, but to avoid them altogether; and if we observe the apostle's precept (Titus 3:8) to be careful to maintain good works, we shall find ourselves far too much occupied with profitable business to take much interest in unworthy, contentious, and needless strivings. There are, however, some questions which are the reverse of foolish, which we must not avoid, but fairly and honestly meet, such as these: Do I believe in the Lord Jesus Christ? Am I renewed in the spirit of my mind? Am I walking, not after the flesh, but after the Spirit? Am I growing in grace? Does my conversation adorn the doctrine of God my Saviour? Am I looking for the coming of the Lord, and watching as a servant should do who expects his master? What more can I do for Jesus?

—CHARLES SPURGEON

PRAYER

Lord God, help this country remember that You reward obedience. Fill us with Your Holy Spirit so that we might obey You more fully. Amen.

RONALD REAGAN'S "TEAR DOWN THIS WALL" SPEECH

June 12, 1987

After Nazi Germany fell at the end of World War II, Western and Soviet powers set up different governments in their occupied zones. West Germany became a capitalist democracy, while East Germany became a socialist state. Many people facing hunger, poverty, and repression in Soviet-controlled East Germany tried to go west, using Berlin as the main crossing. The Soviet Union eventually advised the construction of a wall along the inner German border, restricting movement and threatening escapees with execution. The Berlin Wall, viewed by the West as a symbol of Communist tyranny, stood for nearly three decades. In 1987, President Ronald Reagan visited West Berlin and urged Soviet President Mikhail Gorbachev to remove the wall as a gesture toward progress.

PRAYER

Lord, I pray that I will always be moving forward toward You! Amen.

We welcome change and openness; for we believe that freedom and security go together, that the advance of human liberty can only strengthen the cause of world peace. There is one sign the Soviets can make that would be unmistakable, that would advance dramatically the cause of freedom and peace. General Secretary Gorbachev, if you seek peace, if you seek prosperity for the Soviet Union and Eastern Europe, if you seek liberalization: Come here to this gate. Mr. Gorbachev, open this gate. Mr. Gorbachev, tear down this wall!

DO NOT RELENT

Pray, and let God worry.

—Martin Luther

This is the lesson of the parable in Luke 18:1–8 about the widow. She was so persistent and importunate in her refusal to let go of the judge that he was overpowered and had to help her in spite of himself. How much more, Christ argues there (Luke 18:7), will God give us if He sees that we do not stop praying but go right on knocking so that He has to hear it? This is all the more so because He has promised to do so and shows that such persistence is pleasing to Him. Since your need goes right on knocking, therefore, you go right on knocking, too, and do not relent. . . . By urging you not only to ask but also to knock, God intends to test you to see whether you can hold on tight, and to teach you that your prayer is not displeasing to Him or unheard, simply because His answer is delayed and you are permitted to go on seeking and knocking.

—ADAPTED FROM MARTIN LUTHER

PRAYER

Lord, I knock on Your door, and I keep on knocking until I hear from You. Help me to be patient, yet persistent, as I wait for Your answer. Amen.

LET GO AND LET GOD

The cost of freedom is always high—and Americans have always paid it. And one path we shall never choose, and that is the path of surrender or submission.

—John F. Kennedy

In our imperfect condition both of faith and of understanding, the whole question of asking and receiving must necessarily be surrounded with mist and the possibility of mistake. It can be successfully encountered only by the man who for himself asks and hopes. It lies in too lofty regions and involves too many unknown conditions to be reduced to formulas of ours; for God must do only the best, and man is greater and more needy than himself can know.

—GEORGE MACDONALD

PRAYER

Lord, thank You that there is much value in speaking to You and directing my heart toward You. Amen.

THE PRELUDE OF GREAT MERCY

Sincerity moves you in all simplicity to open your heart to God.

—John Bunyan

Prayer is the forerunner of mercy. Turn to sacred history, and you will find that scarcely ever did a great mercy come to this world unheralded by supplication. You have found this true in your own personal experience.

God has given you many an unsolicited favor, but still great prayer has always been the prelude of great mercy with you. When you first found peace through the blood of the cross, you had been praying much, and earnestly interceding with God that he would remove your doubts, and deliver you from your distresses.

Your assurance was the result of prayer. When at any time you have had high and rapturous joys, you have been obliged to look upon them as answers to your prayers. When you have had great deliverances out of sore troubles, and mighty helps in great dangers, you have been able to say, "I sought the Lord, and he heard me, and delivered me from all my fears" [Psalm 34:4].

Prayer is always the preface to blessing. It goes before the blessing as the blessing's shadow. When the sunlight of God's mercies rises upon our necessities, it casts the shadow of prayer far down upon the plain.

—CHARLES SPURGEON

PRAYER

Lord, thank You for the mercy given to me! Thank You for the mercy given to this country. I pray we will seek You first. Amen.

DIFFICULT PRAYER

The secret of my success? It is simple. It is found in the Bible, "In all thy ways acknowledge Him and He shall direct thy paths."

—George Washington Carver

Have you ever noticed how much difficulties play a part in our life? They call forth our power as nothing else can. They strengthen character. . . .

Imagine what the result would be if the child of God had only to kneel down, ask, get, and go away. Loss to the spiritual life would result. Through difficulties we discover how little we have of God's Holy Spirit. There we learn our own weakness and yield to the Holy Spirit to pray in us. There we take our place in Christ Jesus and abide in Him as our only plea with the Father. There our own will and strength are crucified. There we rise in Christ to newness of life. Praise God for the need and the difficulty of persistent prayer as one of His choice means of grace.

Think what Jesus owed to the difficulties in His path. He persevered in prayer in Gethsemane and the prince of this world with all his temptation was overcome.

—ADAPTED FROM ANDREW MURRAY

PRAYER

Lord, help this country to persevere in prayer, as Jesus, our blessed example, did before us. Amen.

WHOLLY INTENT ON PRAYER

Whether or not our prayer is heard depends not on the number of words, but on the fervor of our souls.

—John Chrysostom

Let the first rule of right prayer then be, to have our heart and mind framed as becomes those who are entering into converse with God. This we shall accomplish in regard to the mind, if, laying aside carnal thoughts and cares which might interfere with the direct and pure contemplation of God, it not only be wholly intent on prayer, but also, as far as possible, be borne and raided above itself. I do not here insist on a mind so disengaged as to feel none of the gnawing of anxiety; on the contrary, it is by much anxiety that the fervor of prayer is inflamed. Thus we see that the holy servants of God betray great anguish, not to say solicitude, when they cause the voice of complaint to ascend to the Lord from the deep abyss and the jaws of death.

—JOHN CALVIN

PRAYER

Lord, let not the minds of this country wander but instead be placed on Your heart and desires. Amen.

THE FEDERALIST PAPERS: NO. 10

The Union as a Safeguard Against Domestic Faction and Insurrection

Friday, November 23, 1787

By James Madison

To the People of the State of New York:

Among the numerous advantages promised by a well constructed Union, none deserves to be more accurately developed than its tendency to break and control the violence of faction. The friend of popular governments never finds himself so much alarmed for their character and fate, as when he contemplates their propensity to this dangerous vice. He will not fail, therefore, to set a due value on any plan which, without violating the principles to which he is attached, provides a proper cure for it. The instability, injustice, and confusion introduced into the public councils, have, in truth, been the mortal diseases under which popular governments have everywhere perished; as they continue to be the favorite and fruitful topics from which the adversaries to liberty derive their most specious declamations. The valuable improvements made by the American constitutions on the popular models, both ancient and modern, cannot certainly be too much admired; but it would be an unwarrantable partiality, to contend that they have as effectually obviated the danger on this side, as was wished and expected. Complaints are everywhere heard from our most considerate and virtuous citizens, equally the friends of public and private faith, and of public and personal liberty, that our governments are too unstable, that the public good is disregarded in the conflicts of rival parties, and that measures are too often decided, not according to the rules of justice and the rights of the minor party, but by the superior force of an interested and overbearing majority. However anxiously we may wish that these complaints had no foundation, the evidence, of known facts will not permit us to deny that they are in some degree true. It will be found, indeed, on a candid review of our situation, that some of the distresses under which we labor have been erroneously charged on the operation of our governments; but it will be found, at the same time, that other causes will not alone account for many of our heaviest misfortunes; and, particularly, for that prevailing and increasing distrust of public engagements, and alarm for private rights, which are echoed from one end of the continent to the other. These must be chiefly, if not wholly, effects of the unsteadiness and injustice with which a factious spirit has tainted our public administrations.

By a faction, I understand a number of citizens, whether amounting to a majority or a minority of the whole, who are united and actuated by some common impulse of passion, or of interest, adversed to the rights of other citizens, or to the permanent and aggregate interests of the community.

There are two methods of curing the mischiefs of faction: the one, by removing its causes; the other, by controlling its effects.

There are again two methods of removing the causes of faction: the one, by destroying the liberty which is essential to its existence; the other, by giving to every citizen the same opinions, the same passions, and the same interests.

It could never be more truly said than of the first remedy, that it was worse than the disease. Liberty is to faction what air is to fire, an aliment without which it instantly expires. But it could not be less folly to abolish liberty, which is essential to political life, because it nourishes faction, than it would be to wish the annihilation of air, which is essential to animal life, because it imparts to fire its destructive agency.

The second expedient is as impracticable as the first would be unwise. As long as the reason of man continues fallible, and he is at liberty to exercise it, different opinions will be formed. As long as the connection subsists between his reason and his self-love, his opinions and his passions will have a reciprocal influence on each other; and the former will be objects to which the latter will attach themselves. The diversity in the faculties of men, from which the rights of property originate, is not less an insuperable obstacle to a uniformity of interests. The protection of these faculties is the first object of government. From the protection of different and unequal faculties of acquiring property, the possession of different degrees and kinds of property immediately results; and from the influence of these on the sentiments and views of the respective proprietors, ensues a division of the society into different interests and parties.

The latent causes of faction are thus sown in the nature of man; and we see them everywhere brought into different degrees of activity, according to the different circumstances of civil society. A zeal for different opinions concerning religion, concerning government, and many other points, as well of speculation as of practice; an attachment to different leaders ambitiously contending for pre-eminence and power; or to persons of other descriptions whose fortunes have been interesting to the human passions, have, in turn, divided mankind into parties, inflamed them with mutual animosity, and rendered them much more disposed to vex and oppress each other than to co-operate for their common good. So strong is this propensity of mankind to fall into mutual animosities, that where no substantial occasion presents itself, the most frivolous and fanciful distinctions have been sufficient to kindle their unfriendly passions and excite their most violent conflicts. But the most common and durable source of factions has been the various and unequal distribution of property. Those who hold and those who are without property have ever formed distinct interests in society. Those who are creditors, and those who are debtors, fall under a like discrimination. A landed interest, a manufacturing interest, a mercantile interest, a moneyed interest, with many lesser interests, grow up of necessity in civilized nations, and divide them into different classes, actuated by different sentiments and views. The regulation of these various and interfering interests forms the principal task of modern legislation, and involves the spirit of party and faction in the necessary and ordinary operations of the government.

No man is allowed to be a judge in his own cause, because his interest would certainly bias his judgment, and, not improbably, corrupt his integrity. With equal, nay with greater reason, a body of men are unfit to be both judges and parties at the same time; yet what are many of the most important acts of legislation, but so many judicial determinations, not indeed concerning the rights of single persons, but concerning the rights of large bodies of citizens? And what are the different classes of legislators but advocates and parties to the causes which they determine? Is a law proposed concerning private debts? It is a question to which the creditors are parties on one side and the debtors on the other. Justice ought to hold the balance between them. Yet the parties are, and must be, themselves the judges; and the most numerous party, or, in other words, the most powerful faction must be expected to prevail. Shall domestic manufactures be encouraged, and in what degree, by restrictions on foreign manufactures? are questions which would be differently decided by the landed and the manufacturing classes, and probably by neither with a sole regard to justice and the public good. The apportionment of taxes on the various descriptions of property is an act which seems to require the most exact impartiality; yet there is, perhaps, no legislative act in which greater opportunity and temptation are given to a predominant party to trample on the rules of justice. Every shilling with which they overburden the inferior number, is a shilling saved to their own pockets.

It is in vain to say that enlightened statesmen will be able to adjust these clashing interests, and render them all subservient to the public good. Enlightened statesmen will not always be at the helm. Nor, in many cases, can such an adjustment be made at all without taking into view indirect and remote considerations, which will rarely prevail over the immediate interest which one party may find in disregarding the rights of another or the good of the whole.

The inference to which we are brought is, that the **CAUSES** of faction cannot be removed, and that relief is only to be sought in the means of controlling its **EFFECTS**.

If a faction consists of less than a majority, relief is supplied by the republican principle, which enables the majority to defeat its sinister views by regular vote. It may clog the administration, it may convulse the society; but it will be unable to execute and mask its violence under the forms of the Constitution. When a majority is included in a faction, the form of popular government, on the other hand, enables it to sacrifice to its ruling passion or interest both the public good and the rights of other citizens. To secure the public good and private rights against the danger of such a faction, and at the same time to preserve the spirit and the form of popular government, is then the great object to which our inquiries are directed. Let me add that it is the great desideratum by which this form of government can be rescued from the opprobrium under which it has so long labored, and be recommended to the esteem and adoption of mankind.

By what means is this object attainable? Evidently by one of two only. Either the existence of the same passion or interest in a majority at the same time must be prevented, or the majority, having such coexistent passion or interest, must be rendered, by their number and local situation, unable to concert and carry into effect schemes of oppression. If the impulse and the opportunity be suffered to coincide, we well know that neither moral nor religious motives can be relied on as an adequate control. They are not found to be such on the injustice and violence of individuals, and lose their efficacy in proportion to the number combined together, that is, in proportion as their efficacy becomes needful.

From this view of the subject it may be concluded that a pure democracy, by which I mean a society consisting of a small number of citizens, who assemble and administer the government in person, can admit of no cure for the mischiefs of faction. A common passion or interest will, in almost every case, be felt by a majority of the whole; a communication and concert result from the form of government itself; and there is nothing to check the inducements to sacrifice the weaker party or an obnoxious individual. Hence it is that such democracies have ever been spectacles of turbulence and contention; have ever been found incompatible with personal security or the rights of property; and have in general been as short in their lives as they have been violent in their deaths. Theoretic politicians, who have patronized this species of government, have erroneously supposed that by reducing mankind to a perfect equality in their political rights, they would, at the same time, be perfectly equalized and assimilated in their possessions, their opinions, and their passions.

A republic, by which I mean a government in which the scheme of representation takes place, opens a different prospect, and promises the cure for which we are seeking. Let us examine the points in which it varies from pure democracy, and we shall comprehend both the nature of the cure and the efficacy which it must derive from the Union.

The two great points of difference between a democracy and a republic are: first, the delegation of the government, in the latter, to a small number of citizens elected by the rest; secondly, the greater number of citizens, and greater sphere of country, over which the latter may be extended.

The effect of the first difference is, on the one hand, to refine and enlarge the public views, by passing them through the medium of a chosen body of citizens, whose wisdom may best discern the true interest of their country, and whose patriotism and love of justice will be least likely to sacrifice it to temporary or partial considerations. Under such a regulation, it may well happen that the public voice, pronounced by the representatives of the people, will be more consonant to the public good than if pronounced by the people themselves, convened for the purpose. On the other hand, the effect may be inverted. Men of factious tempers, of local prejudices, or of sinister designs, may, by intrigue, by corruption, or by other means, first obtain the suffrages, and then betray the interests, of the people. The question resulting is, whether small or extensive republics are more favorable to the election of proper guardians of the public weal; and it is clearly decided in favor of the latter by two obvious considerations:

In the first place, it is to be remarked that, however small the republic may be, the representatives must be raised to a certain number, in order to guard against the cabals of a few; and that, however large it may be, they must be limited to a certain number, in order to guard against the confusion of a multitude. Hence, the number of representatives in the two cases not being in proportion to that of the two constituents, and being proportionally greater in the small republic, it follows that, if the proportion of fit characters be not less in the large than in the small republic, the former will present a greater option, and consequently a greater probability of a fit choice.

In the next place, as each representative will be chosen by a greater number of citizens in the large than in the small republic, it will be more difficult for unworthy candidates to practice with success the vicious arts by which elections are too often carried; and the suffrages of the people being more free, will be more likely to centre in men who possess the most attractive merit and the most diffusive and established characters.

It must be confessed that in this, as in most other cases, there is a mean, on both sides of which inconveniences will be found to lie. By enlarging too much the number of electors, you render the representatives too little acquainted with all their local circumstances and lesser interests; as by reducing it too much, you render him unduly attached to these, and too little fit to comprehend and pursue great and national objects. The federal Constitution forms a happy combination in this respect; the great and aggregate interests being referred to the national, the local and particular to the State legislatures.

The other point of difference is, the greater number of citizens and extent of territory which may be brought within the compass of republican than of democratic government; and it is this circumstance principally which renders factious combinations less to be dreaded in the former than in the latter. The smaller the society, the fewer probably will be the distinct parties and interests composing it; the fewer the distinct parties and interests, the more frequently will a majority be found of the same party; and the smaller the number of individuals composing a majority, and the smaller the compass within which they are placed, the more easily will they concert and execute their plans of oppression. Extend the sphere, and you take in a greater variety of parties and interests; you make it less probable that a majority of the whole will have a common motive to invade the rights of other citizens; or if such a common motive exists, it will be more difficult for all who feel it to discover their own strength, and to act in unison with each other. Besides other impediments, it may be remarked that, where there is a consciousness of unjust or dishonorable purposes, communication is always checked by distrust in proportion to the number whose concurrence is necessary.

Hence, it clearly appears, that the same advantage which a republic has over a democracy, in controlling the effects of faction, is enjoyed by a large over a small republic,—is enjoyed by the Union over the States composing it. Does the advantage consist in the substitution of representatives whose enlightened views and virtuous sentiments render them superior to local prejudices and schemes of injustice? It will not be denied that the representation of the Union will be most likely to possess these requisite endowments. Does it consist in the greater security afforded by a greater variety of parties, against the event of any one party being able to outnumber and oppress the rest? In an equal degree does the increased variety of parties comprised within the Union, increase this security. Does it, in fine, consist in the greater obstacles opposed to the concert and accomplishment of the secret wishes of an unjust and interested majority? Here, again, the extent of the Union gives it the most palpable advantage.

The influence of factious leaders may kindle a flame within their particular States, but will be unable to spread a general conflagration through the other States. A religious sect may degenerate into a political faction in a part of the

Confederacy; but the variety of sects dispersed over the entire face of it must secure the national councils against any danger from that source. A rage for paper money, for an abolition of debts, for an equal division of property, or for any other improper or wicked project, will be less apt to pervade the whole body of the Union than a particular member of it; in the same proportion as such a malady is more likely to taint a particular county or district, than an entire State.

In the extent and proper structure of the Union, therefore, we behold a republican remedy for the diseases most incident to republican government. And according to the degree of pleasure and pride we feel in being republicans, ought to be our zeal in cherishing the spirit and supporting the character of Federalists.

PUBLIUS.

PUTTING YOURSELF IN GOD'S PRESENCE

Freedom of religion; freedom of the press, and freedom of person under the protection of the habeas corpus, and trial by juries impartially selected. These principles . . . guided our steps through an age of revolution and reformation.

—Thomas Jefferson

Perhaps you are not able to pray silently. Many people today are poor at this. Here is an easy way to get started. There are several ways you can place yourself in God's presence.

Consider how God is present in all things and in all places. . . . Since we can't see God physically present, we need to activate our consciousness. Before praying, we need to remind ourselves of God's actual presence. A good way to do this is with Bible verses. "If I ascend into heaven, You are there; If I make my bed in hell, behold, You are there" (Psalm 139:8 NKJV).

Remember also that God is not only where you are, he is actually in your heart, in the core of your spirit. "For in Him we live and move and have our being" (Acts 17:28 NKJV). . . .

When you know God is present, your soul will bow before his majesty and ask for help. "Do not cast me away from Your presence, And do not take Your Holy Spirit from me" (Psalm 51:11 NKJV).

—ADAPTED FROM SAINT FRANCIS DE SALES

PRAYER

Dear God, when You seem far from me, help me to understand how wonderfully near You truly are. Amen.

HAPPY AND PROSPEROUS

Most of my struggles in the Christian life circle around the same two themes: why God doesn't act the way we want God to, and why I don't act the way God wants me to. Prayer is the precise point where those themes converge.

—Philip Yancey

In his 1801 inaugural address, President Thomas Jefferson offered the following encouragement:

Enlightened by a benign religion, professed, indeed, and practiced in various forms, yet all of them inculcating honesty, truth, temperance, gratitude, and the love of man; acknowledging and adoring an overruling Providence, which by all its dispensations proves that it delights in the happiness of man here and his greater happiness hereafter—with all these blessings, what more is necessary to make us a happy and prosperous people? Still one thing more, fellow-citizens—a wise and frugal Government, which shall restrain men from injuring one another, shall leave them otherwise free to regulate their own pursuits of industry and improvement, and shall not take from the mouth of labor the bread it has earned.

PRAYER

Lord, I pray that my fellow Americans always seek to help others by the gifts that You have given to them. Amen.

PRAYER FOR THE YEARS TO COME

We can be tired, weary and emotionally distraught, but after spending time alone with God, we find that He injects into our bodies energy, power and strength.

—Charles Stanley

Hast thou no mercy to ask of God? Then, may the Lord's mercy show thee thy misery! A prayerless soul is a Christless soul.

Prayer is the lisping of the believing infant, the shout of the fighting believer, the requiem of the dying saint falling asleep in Jesus. It is the breath, the watchword, the comfort, the strength, the honour of a Christian.

If thou be a child of God, thou wilt seek thy Father's face, and live in thy Father's love. Pray that this year thou mayst be holy, humble, zealous and patient; have closer communion with Christ, and enter oftener into the banqueting-house of his love.

Pray that thou mayst be an example and a blessing unto others—and that thou mayst live more to the glory of thy Master. The motto for this year must be, "Continue in prayer" (Colossians 4:2).

—CHARLES SPURGEON

PRAYER

Heavenly Father, my time spent with You is precious. Help me to remember Your instruction to continue in prayer. Amen.

PLEASING THE FATHER

God grants liberty only to those who love it, and are always ready to guard and defend it.

—Daniel Webster

Are we not all too apt to seek Him rather because of our need than for His joy and pleasure? This should not be. We do not admire selfish children who only think of what they can get from their parents, and are unmindful of the pleasure that they may give or the service that they may render. But are not we in danger of forgetting that pleasing God means giving Him pleasure? Some of us look back to the time when the words "To please God" meant no more than not to sin against Him, not to grieve Him; but would the love of earthly parents be satisfied with the mere absence of disobedience? Or a bridegroom, if his bride only sought him for the supply of her own need?

—HUDSON TAYLOR

PRAYER

Lord, I want to please You in every aspect of my life. Do not let anything come between me and Your wonderful presence. Amen.

SCENE OF LOVE FROM PAUL'S JOURNEYS

The object of love is to serve, not to win.

—Woodrow Wilson

Following his visit to Ephesus, [Paul] arrived at Tyre, where he stopped a few days. Here he found some disciples, who begged Paul not to go to Jerusalem, saying through the Spirit that he should not go up to that city. But Paul adhered to his original purpose to go to Jerusalem. The account says: And when we had accomplished those days, we departed, and went our way; and they all brought us on our way with their wive and children, till we were out of the city; and we kneeled down on the shore and prayed.

PRAYER

Heavenly Father, before any venture I make in life, remind me to first spend time with You in prayer. Amen.

What a sight to observe on that seashore. Here is a family picture of love and devotion where husbands, wives, and even children are present, and prayer is made out in the open air. What an impression it must have made upon those children! The vessel was ready to depart, but prayer must cement their affections and sanctify wives and children, and bless their parting—a parting which was to be final so far as this world was concerned. . . .

Never did a sea strand see a grander picture or witness a lovelier sight—Paul on his knees on the sands of that shore, invoking God's blessing upon these men, women, and children.

—E. M. BOUNDS

PRAYER AND FASTING

For this is what America is all about. It is the uncrossed desert and the unclimbed ridge. It is the star that is not reached and the harvest that is sleeping in the unplowed ground.

—Lyndon B. Johnson

Jesus teaches us that a life of faith requires both prayer and fasting. Prayer grasps the power of heaven, fasting loosens the hold on earthly pleasure. . . .

Abstinence from food, or moderation in taking it, helps to focus on communication with God.

Let's remember that abstinence, moderation, and self-denial are a help to the spiritual life. . . . To willingly sacrifice our own pleasure or enjoyment will help to focus our minds more fully on God and His priorities. The very practice needed in overcoming our own desires will give us strength to take hold of God in prayer.

Our lack of discipline in prayer comes from our fleshly desire of comfort and ease. Those who belong to Christ Jesus have nailed the passions and desires of their sinful nature to his cross and crucified them there (Galatians 5:24). . . . For the real practice of prayer—taking hold of God and having communion and fellowship with Him—it is necessary that our selfish desires be sacrificed. Isn't it worth the trouble to deny ourselves daily in order to meet the holy God and receive His blessings?

—ADAPTED FROM ANDREW MURRAY

PRAYER

Heavenly Father, help me to deny my selfish desires and discover the power that fasting can bring to my life. Amen.

WHY, LORD?

The men who have done mighty things for God have always been mighty in prayer.

—E. M. Bounds

'Tis a point I long to know,
Oft it causes anxious thought,
Do I love the Lord, or no?
Am I his, or am I not?
If I love, why am I thus?
Why this dull and lifeless frame?
Hardly, sure, could they be worse,
Who have never heard His name.
Could my heart so hard remain?
Prayer a task and burden prove?
Ev'ry trifle give me pain,
If I knew a Saviour's love?
When I turn my eyes within,
All is dark and vain and wild;
Fill'd with unbelief and sin,
Can a deem myself a child?
If I pray, or hear, or read,
Sin is mix'd with all I do.
You that love the Lord indeed,
Tell me, is it thus with you?
Yet I mourn my stubborn will.
Find my sin a grief and thrall:
Should I grieve for what I feel,
If I did not love at all?

—JOHN NEWTON

PRAYER

Lord, hear these words that I pray aloud. Maybe I be convicted when I do not love You and others. Amen.

OUR NEEDS

Better, though difficult, the right way to go, Than wrong, though easy, where the end is woe.

—John Bunyan, *The Pilgrim's Progress*

In asking we must always truly feel our wants, and seriously considering that we need all the things which we ask, accompany the prayer with a sincere, nay, ardent desire of obtaining them. Many repeat prayers in a perfunctory manner from a set form, as if they were performing a task to God, and though they confess that this is a necessary remedy for the evils of their condition, because it were fatal to be left without the divine aid which they implore, it still appears that they perform the duty from custom, because their minds are meanwhile cold, and they ponder not what they ask. A general and confused feeling of their necessity leads them to pray, but it does not make them solicitous as in a matter of present consequence, that they may obtain the supply of their need.

—JOHN CALVIN

PRAYER

Lord, may the words of my mouth and the meditation of my heart today be pleasing to You. Amen.

A WILLING MAN

Nothing binds me to my Lord like a strong belief in His changeless love.

—Charles Spurgeon

Agricultural chemist George Washington Carver discovered over three hundred uses for peanuts and hundreds more uses for soybeans, pecans, and sweet potatoes. When asked for his thoughts about God, he said:

As a very small boy exploring the almost virgin woods of the old Carver place I had the impression someone had just been there ahead of me. Things were so orderly, so clean, so harmoniously beautiful. A few years later in this same woods . . . I was practically overwhelmed with the sense of some Great Presence. Not only had someone been there. Someone was there. . . .

Years later when I read in the Scriptures, "In Him we live and move and have our being," I knew what the writer meant. Never since have I been without this consciousness of the Creator speaking to me. . . . The out of doors has been to me more and more a great cathedral in which God could be continuously spoken to and heard from. . . .

Man, who needed a purpose, a mission, to keep him alive, had one. He could be . . . God's co-worker. . . . My purpose alone must be God's purpose—to increase the welfare and happiness of His people.

PRAYER

Lord, this country is blessed with the gifts You have given us. Thank You for providing! Amen.

HIGHEST HOPES

Prayer is the core of our day. Take prayer out, and the day would collapse, would be pithless, a straw blown in the wind.

—Amy Carmichael

Daniel Webster, a US congressman and senator, as well as secretary of state for three different presidents, was considered one of the greatest orators in American history. On February 23, 1852, he spoke about the importance of the Christian faith.

If we and our posterity shall be true to the Christian religion, if we and they shall live always in the fear of God, and shall respect his commandments, if we and they shall maintain just moral sentiments and such conscientious convictions of duty as shall control the heart and life, we may have the highest hopes of the future fortunes of our country; . . . but if we and our posterity reject religious instruction and authority, violate the rules of eternal justice, trifle with the injunctions of morality, and recklessly destroy the political constitution which holds us together, no man can tell how sudden a catastrophe may overwhelm us.

PRAYER

Lord, may this country remember why our faith is so important. Amen.

TO GOD BE THE GLORY

This is my story, this is my song,
Praising my Savior all the day long;
This is my story, this is my song,
Praising my Savior all the day long.

—Fanny Crosby

Frances "Fanny" Crosby, one of the most prolific hymn writers in Christian history, was just six weeks old when she lost her sight due to a medical error. Raised by her devout mother and grandmother, she had memorized large portions of the Bible by the age of fifteen.

Building on this strong spiritual foundation, Fanny attended the New York Institute for the Blind, not only as a student, but later as a teacher. Her talent for poetry flourished. In her forties, she began writing hymns. Working with composers like Ira D. Sankey, she created over eight thousand hymns and gospel songs. Her best-known hymns include "Blessed Assurance," "To God Be the Glory," and "Safe in the Arms of Jesus."

Crosby didn't consider her blindness to be a disadvantage, believing the first face she would ever see would be her Savior's in heaven. In addition to her musical legacy, she was passionate about urban mission work, advocating for New York City's poor and marginalized.

Though Fanny Crosby passed away in 1915, her legacy endures. Her beloved hymns continue to echo in churches and gatherings worldwide, firmly cementing her as a truly influential figure in Christian music.

PRAYER

Lord, may the words I use be the sound of worship to Your ears. Amen.

DIVINE PROVIDENCE

A comprehended God is no God.

—**John Chrysostom**

Patrick Henry, a fervent advocate of the Revolutionary War, was known for condemning government corruption and defending colonists' rights. His fiery oratory likened him to an Old Testament prophet. Elected to the Virginia legislature in 1775, he urged the colony to prepare for war.

As tensions rose and Britain increased its military presence in response to tax protests, the Second Virginia Convention met to choose between independence and negotiation. On March 23, 1775, Henry delivered a moving speech, trusting in divine providence. He famously declared:

Sirs, we shall not fight our battles alone. There is a just God who presides over the destinies of nations, and who will raise up friends to fight our battles for us. The battle, sir, is not to the strong alone; it is to the vigilant, the active, the brave. . . .

Is life so dear, or peace so sweet, as to be purchased at the price of chains and slavery? Forbid it, Almighty God! I know not what course others may take; but as for me, give me liberty or give me death!

PRAYER

Lord, we give You thanks for the peace that comes only through You. Amen.

BY DESIGN

Out of him we have all come, in him we are all enfolded and towards him we are all journeying.

—Julian of Norwich

Wernher von Braun, former director of NASA and "Father of the American Space Program," wrote an article titled "My Faith: A Space-Age Scientist Tells Why He Must Believe in God" in 1963, in which he argued that science and religion are complementary, not opposing forces. He believed that studying God's creation through science and understanding the Creator through religion are two separate paths to the same truth.

[This] ultimately raises the question of a Designer. . . . The scientific method does not allow us to exclude data which lead to the conclusion that the universe, life and man are based on design. To be forced to believe only one conclusion—that everything in the universe happened by chance—would violate the very objectivity of science itself. Certainly there are those who argue that the universe evolved out of a random process, but what random process could produce the brain of a man or the system of the human eye?

Many intelligent men say they cannot visualize a Designer. Well, can a physicist visualize an electron? . . . What strange rationale makes some physicists accept the inconceivable electron as real while refusing to accept the reality of a Designer on the ground that they cannot conceive Him?

PRAYER

Lord, thank You for the stars above and the earth below. What wonders You have given us! Amen.

A SIMPLE MESSAGE

Prayer then, purely directed from a faithful heart, riseth like incense from a hallowed altar.

—Saint Augustine

Benjamin Franklin Butler, who served as United States attorney general under President Andrew Jackson, understood the transformative power of faith. Butler wrote:

He is truly happy, whatever may be his temporal condition, who can call God his Father in the full assurance of faith and hope. And amid all his trials, conflicts, and doubts, the feeblest Christian is still comparatively happy; because cheered by the hope . . . that the hour is coming when he shall be delivered from "this body of sin and death" and in the vision of his Redeemer . . . approximate to the . . . felicity of angels.

Not only does the Bible inculcate, with sanctions of the highest import, a system of the purest morality, but in the person and character of our Blessed Saviour it exhibits a tangible illustration of that system.

In Him we have set before us . . . a model of feeling and action, adapted to all times, places, and circumstances; and combining so much of wisdom, benevolence, and holiness, that none can fathom its sublimity; and yet, presented in a form so simple, that even a child may be made to understand and taught to love it.

PRAYER

Lord, may I come to You always with a childlike faith! Amen.

THE HEIGHT OF HIS LOVE

Prayer is a powerful thing; for God hath bound and tied himself thereunto.

—Martin Luther

The love of Christ in its sweetness, its fulness, its greatness, its faithfulness, passeth all human comprehension. Where shall language be found which shall describe his matchless, his unparalleled love? . . .

For this love of Christ is indeed measureless and fathomless; none can attain unto it. Before we can have any right idea of the love of Jesus, we must understand his previous glory in its height of majesty, and his incarnation upon the earth in all its depths of shame.

But who can tell us the majesty of Christ? When he was enthroned in the highest heavens he was very God of very God; by him were the heavens made, and all the hosts thereof. . . .

Who can tell his height of glory then? And who, on the other hand, can tell how low he descended? To be a man was something, to be a man of sorrows was far more; to bleed, and die, and suffer, these were much for him who was the Son of God; but to suffer such unparalleled agony—to endure a death of shame and desertion by his Father, this is a depth of condescending love which the most inspired mind must utterly fail to fathom.

—CHARLES SPURGEON

PRAYER

Lord, thank You for hearing our prayers! Thank You for the cross and for the many freedoms we have been given. Amen.